Walking on Water

Overcoming the obstacles to the supernatural life

Paul & Becky Harcourt

RIVER
PUBLISHING

River Publishing & Media Ltd
Bradbourne Stables
East Malling
Kent ME19 6DZ
United Kingdom

info@river-publishing.co.uk

Published in partnership with New Wine Trust
www.new-wine.org

MIX
Paper from
responsible sources
FSC® C117931

ISBN 978-1-908393-71-5
Cover design by www.spiffingcovers.com
Printed and bound by MBM Print SCS Ltd, Glasgow

Contents

What Others Are Saying...

"Paul and Becky are heroes of the faith in every sense of the word. They live what they preach and it gives their words a power and profoundness that can't be manufactured. *Walking on Water* is a testament to the grace and greatness of God, lived out in the lives of ordinary people facing real and difficult challenges. The pages of this book will inspire and encourage you to keep going, keep growing, keep moving towards the finish line, knowing that with Christ all things are possible."
Arianna Walker, Chief Executive of Mercy UK

"Real. Raw. True. Paul and Becky open up to give us the keys to living the naturally-supernatural life. Permit their story access to your heart and soul, so that the Spirit may challenge you to get out of the boat and begin living the life abundant. They are the real deal ... and here are their keys."
Rob Peabody, Founder & CEO, Awaken Movement

"In coming years, it is vital for the strength of the Church for believers to have a genuine depth to their faith, and that we allow God to stretch and grow us as we yield to his goodness. What I love about Paul and Becky Harcourt is that they have that depth – they are solid. Solid in their faith, in their way of life, in their discipleship. They model what it looks like to follow hard after Christ, even in the most difficult of circumstances.

I have no doubt that you will be challenged and thoroughly encouraged by Walking on Water."
Christy Wimber, Pastor, Author, Church Planter, Speaker.

"A wonderful, inspiring book that tackles head-on some of the issues that stop us becoming all we can be in Jesus. Buy it, read it, live it, and overcome the obstacles that can so easily hold us back."
Gavin Calver, Director of Mission, Evangelical Alliance

"I have had the honour of getting to know Paul and Becky over the last few years and they are people of abounding love, integrity and grace. As you read the honest and inspiring account of their own personal journey in this book, you too will be challenged and encouraged to dare to journey – into the depths of God's healing life, love and presence, which brings great freedom and will propel you deeper into all He has called you to be. I cannot recommend it highly enough!"
Nicola Neal, Founder and CEO, Revelation Life

"This is a book that deserves to be read by those who struggle to embrace and live the Spirit-led, supernatural life, and all those who wish to help them. It is profound in its content, accessible in its style, and inspiring in its vulnerability. The thesis that some struggle because of 'mental blocks' and others because of 'heart trouble' rings true to life and pastoral ministry. *Walking on Water* will encourage, reassure, help and

challenge the reader to accept Jesus' invitation to take steps into the supernatural. Buy it now – to read or give away!"
John Dunnett, General Director, CPAS

"How refreshing to read a book by two gifted leaders who are willing to take us beyond their visible ministry into places we rarely see. Paul and Becky's vulnerability will undoubtedly move you, and their practical and thought-provoking teaching will equip you as a disciple. But, most of all, the wisdom in these pages will build your faith and cause your soul to sing, even when the going gets tough."
Cathy Madavan, Speaker, Writer, member of Spring Harvest Planning Group and author of *Digging for Diamonds*.

"Paul and Becky's powerful personal stories encourage us to press through the constraints of intellectual doubt, personal disappointment and overwhelming fear, confident that we too can encounter the Holy Spirit at work in and through our lives, in surprising and extraordinary ways."
Rev Dr Kate Coleman, Founder and co-director of Next Leadership

Grateful Thanks...

...to all those who have helped us overcome our own barriers.

...and those whose love and support for our family enables us to go out and help others overcome theirs (you know who you are!)

...to the congregations associated with All Saints' Woodford Wells and to New Wine friends near and far.

Chapter 1
An Invitation Into the Impossible

James Irwin walked on the Moon, and while he was there, he met God.

The American astronaut, in fact the eighth man to walk on the Moon but the first to drive the famous Lunar Rover Moon buggy, was struggling to erect the equipment needed for a vital experiment. Unbeknownst to him, his heart rate was also fluctuating in a manner that was causing concern in Mission Control back on Earth, due to a kink in the tube feeding him water. Despite being only a nominal Christian who had wandered away from his religious upbringing, he decided to pray and ask God for wisdom. In a matter of moments, the obstinate equipment unfolded and was set up. Irwin's wife, Mary, later described how this answer to prayer came with an encounter that changed his life. "He was so overwhelmed at seeing and feeling God's presence so close," she says. "At one point, he turned around and looked over his shoulder as if he was standing there."

His view of the Earth from space, and his encounter with God on the Moon, profoundly affected his life forever. Less than a year after returning from the Moon's surface, James Irwin had left NASA to found the High Flight Foundation, dedicated to telling as many people as possible about Jesus. Famously, he said, "God decided that he would send his Son Jesus Christ to the blue planet … Jesus walking on the Earth is more important than man walking on the Moon."

For those of us who believe that Jesus is indeed God incarnate, God with us in the flesh, that statement holds great meaning. God sent his only Son to become one of us in order that we might be restored into relationship with him and receive his life – that is the heart of our faith. We believe that Jesus was unlike anyone who ever came before, or has come since.

But he wasn't completely unlike us. An essential element of Christian faith is the assertion that Jesus was and is fully God, but that he was also fully human. He voluntarily limited himself from using characteristics that were inherent in his divinity, without ever ceasing to be God. Jesus embraced our humanity fully, so that, whilst he was walking amongst us, he suffered pain, tiredness, and hunger – all the weaknesses that are part of the human experience. He laid aside his omniscience (complete knowledge of everything) and had to ask questions. He faced – and overcame – temptation, for us and our benefit: *"we do not have a high priest who is unable to empathise with our weaknesses, but we have one who has been tempted in every way, just as we are—yet he did not sin"* (Hebrews 4:15). And, crucially, his embrace of the human condition meant that he laid aside his omnipotence (the quality of being all-powerful). Jesus performed no miracles, except in obedience to his Father and in dependence on the power of the Holy Spirit.

"Very truly I tell you, the Son can do nothing by himself; he can do only what he sees his Father doing, because whatever the Father does the Son also does." (John 5:19)

In a similar way, Jesus says later, *"I do nothing on my own but speak just what the Father has taught me"* (John 8:28). Neither statement in any way takes away from the truth of Jesus' identity as the unique and eternal Son of God, but they say something very important about his identity as the Son of Man. Jesus shows us what the Father is like, but it is just as true to say that he also shows us what *we* can be like. Although we will never achieve that perfection in this life, Jesus' example is in every way the benchmark towards which the Spirit is trying to lift us.

That's why, from the beginning of his ministry, Jesus sought to involve the disciples in signs, wonders and miracles. In my first book, *Growing in Circles*, I drew attention to the way in which Jesus trained his disciples in a supernatural ministry of healing and deliverance to demonstrate the love of God and the nature of the Kingdom that he was bringing. This begins right from the initial choice of the disciples, where it says, *"he appointed twelve, that they might be with him and that he might send them out to preach and have authority to drive out demons"* (Mark 3:14-15). Being a disciple of Jesus meant learning to do the things that he did. The rest of *Growing in Circles*[1] was an attempt to draw out some principles as to how we can grow in that amazing calling through understanding our identity as adopted sons and daughters of God. If Jesus did those things simply because he was God, then he could not have passed them on to his disciples, then or now.

These truths, of Jesus' identity as both God and man, and of his calling us to enter into his own experience, come together in one of the most well-known Bible stories, when Jesus walks on water and Peter tries to do the same (Matthew 14:22-33). If the greatest news that we could ever receive is that God has walked on Earth, it would be no surprise that he could also walk on water. As Jared Wilson quips in his book, *The Wonder Working God*, Jesus walking on water is merely, "walking around as if he made the place."[2] However, what constitutes one of the greatest challenges that we could ever receive is that Peter also walked on the water! An ordinary human being, like you and me, certainly not divine and more often known for his weaknesses than his strengths, steps out of the boat at Jesus' invitation and finds that the water bears him up as well. I find that profoundly encouraging, as well as profoundly challenging.

Let's consider that story in more detail. It comes

12

immediately after Jesus had heard of the martyrdom of his cousin, John the Baptist, and had withdrawn from the crowds to find a solitary place for prayer. However, the crowds would not let him escape that easily and followed him into that remote place, with the day drawing to a close and no food to sustain them. Though they had brought this on themselves, Jesus takes the little food that the disciples bring to him, blesses it and directs them to distribute it amongst the crowd. As they did this, somehow everyone received sufficient to eat, with an impossible amount left over! Although he was the source of the miracle, it seems that it took place in the hands of the disciples as they broke the bread and fish. They were left to ponder the meaning of what they had just experienced as Jesus sent them away across the lake in a boat and dismissed the crowd, that he might finally have some quiet in which to pray.

The lake in this instance was the Sea of Galilee, a large freshwater lake, surrounded on several sides by a ring of hills and valleys. After the Dead Sea, it is also the second lowest lake in the world and relatively shallow. When combined with the temperature differential between the seacoast and the mountains, the result is that strong winds often fall from the heights to the sea, funneled through the hills. As the lake is both small and shallow, the winds can descend directly onto the centre of the Sea of Galilee with violent results. Whipped up in a matter of minutes, storms come without warning. With several experienced fishermen amongst their number, the disciples knew the danger that they faced and were already getting nervous as their boat was *"buffeted by the waves"* (verse 24).

It was in that precarious state, and in the twilight before dawn, that they saw a figure moving across the water.

One issue that we all face when confronted with something outside of our previous experience is that we are naturally afraid. As we read the passage, and knowing the identity of the man who is walking across the lake, it's easy to be critical of the disciples for their reaction. *"'It's a ghost', they said and cried out in fear"* (verse 26). We reason that they should have recognised Jesus, or that they should have been more open to supernatural phenomena, having just participated in the miraculous multiplication of food.

Yet, if we're honest, our own responses to things beyond our understanding are often remarkably similar. When God shows up in our lives (or in our churches) in a manner that we've not seen before, people react in the same way the disciples did. Christians have often been disturbed by the physical manifestations that sometimes accompany a move of the Spirit, such as people falling, crying out or shaking violently. We say things such as, "This cannot be God because I feel afraid" – even though that is exactly what the disciples felt that day! Or we misinterpret what is going on: "I've known God for a long time and I've never seen this before, therefore this isn't God." The disciples, having not seen Jesus walk on water before, concluded that what they were seeing was a ghost. Sometimes, tragically I believe, the Church in many parts has concluded that an unusual move of God in our midst was instead actually the work of the Enemy. These are only natural human reactions, but they are ones of which we should we aware, lest we miss the wonderful, eye-opening things that come from following a God who is always greater, beyond anything we have, to that date, experienced. When we give it even a moment's thought, it is surely foolish to believe that we've seen enough of God to have seen everything that he might do.

As we assess spiritual things, which we are indeed called to do (1 John 4:1, 1 Thessalonians 5:21 etc), it's important to remember that God's intention is never to leave us guessing or to frighten us. Just as the angels always seem to open their conversations with people in the Bible by saying, *"Do not be afraid"*, Jesus also immediately said to the twelve, *"Take courage! It is I. Do not be afraid"* (verse 27). When God comes close, we may experience fear, but we should also expect to hear words of reassurance. In the end, all we need to know is that it is him.

Peter has often been stereotyped by popular Christian preaching as something of a buffoon, a comical figure who speaks first and thinks later, who jumps into situations without considering the consequences. That has its origin in the portrayal of the disciples in the gospels, especially in the Gospel of Mark (for which many scholars believe Peter was a main source). The disciples, eyewitnesses of Jesus' glory, were at pains to ensure that Christianity would only ever have one hero, Jesus. They described in unflinching detail their sins and faults, and how they failed so often to grasp the truths that Jesus was trying to teach them. So, we remember that Peter got many things wrong, trying to turn Jesus from the path of the cross, denying him when he was arrested, and struggling to believe that he could be forgiven after the resurrection.

Yet, Peter also got many things right. He was first to grasp Jesus' true identity at Caesarea Philippi, first into the tomb, first to preach at Pentecost. Peter is, in many ways, the paradigm disciple. He stands out because of the greatness of his heart and the boldness of his faith. Though by no means perfect, Peter so often shows us the way and is first to walk it with Jesus. On the Sea of Galilee that day, confronted with something for which he had no frame of reference, Peter blurted out, *"Lord, if it is you, tell me to come to you on the water"* (verse 28).

The answer that he received was simple. One word. *"Come,"* Jesus said.

Over the past few years, I have thought many times about that one word. It's a word full of grace and invitation. Jesus could easily have rebuked Peter for questioning and demanding proof that it was him, but he didn't. We might also expect Jesus to point out that people don't normally walk on water, so who did Peter think Jesus was? More pointedly, by asking to come onto the water and join him, wasn't Peter thinking rather highly of himself?! Either answer would make sense within the framework of the theologies which most of us believe. Yet we cannot escape the fact that Jesus invited Peter out of the boat and onto the surface of the lake. That means that there was an invitation to step into the impossible – not just to witness Jesus performing miracles, but to join with him and step into a supernatural experience of life.

I've grown to believe that Jesus' invitation to Peter is, in fact, an invitation to us all. All disciples are called to join with Jesus in a lifestyle of walking with God, which includes miracles, signs and wonders. It is interesting to me that the gospels don't seem to make much of this incident. It seems more miraculous and more dramatic even than the feeding of the 5000, which is mentioned in all four gospels and frequently referred to after it has taken place.

By contrast, although included by Matthew, Mark and John, this amazing story is not mentioned at all by Luke, and only Matthew talks about Peter's experience. Perhaps the reason that only one gospel includes this remarkable aspect is precisely that it *was* so dramatic – the first disciples and the early Church didn't want those that came after them to make "water walking" into a test of faith (like some fringe Christian groups have done with "snake handling"). My conclusion is that this story, witnessed only by the disciples and not by the crowds, in many ways repeats and sums up the lessons that they were receiving about moving in the supernatural throughout their time with Jesus. It wasn't about the specifics of the miracle, more about its meaning in the context of being a disciple. Whilst they were in the boat and apart from Jesus, they were making slow progress and fearing that they would be overwhelmed. When he appeared, everything changed. A miracle took place before their very eyes, they knew that Jesus was indeed with them, and we read, *"the wind died down"* (verse 32) and *"they worshipped him"* (verse 33).

But what if Peter had never left the boat? After all, none of the others did. If Jesus' invitation out onto the water is a helpful metaphor for his invitation to all disciples to join him in something more, then putting ourselves into Peter's shoes will enable us to face the issues in our own lives that prevent us from following Jesus and experiencing signs and wonders. Simply put, it seems to me that there would be two main obstacles that could have prevented Peter from stepping out of the boat – his *head* and his *heart.* These represent two great barriers to entering into more with God. The first is all about the rational mind and the demand to understand before we experience. The second revolves more around the woundedness of our hearts, which leads to the fear of being let down and the conclusion that we must never take risks. Both ultimately express a desire to remain in control, and so both prevent the faith that steps out into what appears impossible.

Becky and I have taught from this passage on several

occasions over the past couple of years. Each time we have done so, we've seen new details and further applications of Peter's experience to our own lives. It helps that Becky and I are quite different in our personalities and ways of seeing the world. We've come to appreciate those differences, and realise that sharing from our very different perspectives often enables more people to make connections with what we're saying. Our expectation is that, as you read this book, you'll be able to relate to some chapters more than others. However, we hope that each chapter will have something to say to everyone. Each of us has issues both with our heads and our hearts. Becky and I have drawn on our own individual experiences and want to share something of our stories, but we've also learnt a lot from each other.

My story has more to do with overcoming the rational mind's refusal to embrace what it cannot fully comprehend, and Becky's story is a powerful testimony of God healing her heart after a succession of tragedies in her family history. We are all born favouring a certain way of seeing the world, but whatever the science behind what are popularly known as "left and right brain" genetic predispositions, our path through life will have left all of us with issues in both areas. Whereas *Growing in Circles* was a reflection on the dynamic cycle of grace that enables us to grow into a deeper experience of truly charismatic discipleship, this book focuses more on the obstacles to that adventure that we might face from our personality types and inherited preferences, our early development, and our subsequent life experiences. It's a journey that we're still on, and joyfully know that we'll spend our whole lives exploring.

So, before you read any further, can I suggest that you pause for a quiet moment? Deep down, I believe that everyone who is following Jesus knows that there is more to life than they are currently experiencing. We all know that God is more wonderful in his ways than we have yet seen. It is in the heart of every believer to hunger for more of his presence and a closer walk with him, even if sometimes our heads have rationalised that what we have already known must be all that there is. You may have had a sense on many occasions that Jesus is inviting you to more, perhaps with frustration over not then experiencing it. I pray that there might be something in these pages that would strike a chord with you, or offer another perspective that would help you receive from the Lord.

Listen for Jesus' invitation. To each of us, he says simply, "*Come.*"

You are invited to walk on the water with him.

Endnotes
1. *Growing in Circles* by Paul Harcourt, New Wine/River Publishing (2016)
2. *The Wonder Working God* (Chapter 4) by Jared C. Wilson, Crossway (2014)

"Mental Blocks"

What if Peter refused to step out of the boat until he understood how it could be possible for water to hold him up?

―∾―

Paul's Story

Chapter 2
Trust and Obey

Since Sir Arthur Conan Doyle created him in 1887, Sherlock Holmes has been portrayed by over 75 actors on our screens, including Sir Christopher Lee, Charlton Heston, Peter O'Toole, Peter Cook, Roger Moore, and, more recently, Benedict Cumberbatch and Robert Downey Jr. With 254 separate depictions, the Guinness World Records organisation have officially crowned him with the world record for the most portrayed literary human character in film and TV. Guinness World Records adjudicator Claire Burgess commented, "Sherlock Holmes is a literary institution. This Guinness World Records title reflects his enduring appeal and demonstrates that his detective talents are as compelling today as they were 125 years ago." Through a combination of films, television series, dramas and documentaries, Sherlock's appearances beat the character of Shakespeare's Hamlet by 48 portrayals to claim the title.[1]

Why is it that Sherlock has such enduring appeal? Could it be that, in this complicated and confusing world, we are attracted to the idea that at least one person can sort through all the data and make sense of the chaos? For all his flaws, Sherlock Holmes commands respect because he seems to see through to the heart of the matter.

As I've mentioned already, Peter is often described to us in terms of his flaws – but there are also some wonderful strengths that he embodies. Far from being a bumbling fool who is constantly getting things wrong, I think we should honour Peter for being the one who often gets it right, not least in receiving revelation and grasping the true identity of his Lord. It would be John who in time became the theologian, reflecting deeply on the mystery of Jesus' nature, but at times in the gospels it is actually Peter who gets to a true understanding first. At Caesarea Philippi, it was Peter who first declared the identity of Jesus (*"You are the Messiah, the Son of the living God"* – Matthew 16:16). On the Mount of Transfiguration, although he is, understandably, overwhelmed by the glory shining from Jesus' face and clothes and the appearance of ancient biblical heroes, long dead, Peter correctly identifies Moses and Elijah as the figures standing with Jesus. Both these events occur later in the gospel than the incident on which we're focusing.

But one other significant moment of Peter receiving revelation seems particularly relevant, and comes earlier. In Luke 5:1-11, the disciples were cleaning their nets after a night of fishing. This was usually done in the midday sun, so that the nets dried as they were washed. It had been a frustrating night, where they'd returned empty handed. As they worked though, Jesus commandeered Peter's boat as a sort of mobile pulpit, pushing out from shore and putting a little distance between himself and the crowd. After he'd finished teaching, Jesus turned to Peter and said, *"Put out into the deep water, and let down the nets for a catch"* (Luke 5:4). It doesn't require much knowledge of fishing to realise that this was an unusual request. The nets would need to be untangled and cleaned all over again, after what would almost certainly be another fruitless trip. Fishermen want the fish to be active and feeding near the surface – you caught fish at night, in shallow water, not in the daytime in deep water!

Almost everything in Peter's experience must have screamed that this was a waste of time and effort, but something told him that Jesus was worth obeying. *"Master, we've worked hard all night and haven't caught anything. But because you say so, I will let down the nets"* (verse 5). The result was such a large catch that it took a couple of boats to land it, and even then, they almost sank because of the weight of fish! How often do we need to listen to that little voice telling us that, with Jesus, everything we know can be turned on it's head?

As in the later stories listed above, it is Peter who makes the intuitive leap to a shocking conclusion. *"When Simon*

Peter saw this, he fell at Jesus' knees and said, 'Go away from me, Lord; I am a sinful man!'" (Luke 5:8). The next two verses explicitly state that *"all his companions ... and James and John, the sons of Zebedee, Simon's partners"* were astonished at the miraculous catch of fish ... yet only Peter realised the implications of what he had just experienced.

Let's not think that Peter acts without thinking when, in Matthew 14, he steps out of the boat and walks towards Jesus. You don't even need to be an experienced sailor to know that staying in the boat is required for safety when away from land! Peter isn't acting illogically or irrationally – on the contrary, he is working things through more logically than anyone else in the boat. Note that Peter prefaces his request by saying, *"Lord, if it's you..."*[2] If it truly is Jesus, then the seemingly impossible makes sense, because of who Jesus is. And if Jesus has the authority to command the waves to bear him up, then he has the authority to command them to bear up someone else. Sherlock Holmes is famous for saying, "Eliminate all other factors and the one which remains must be the truth."[3] It seems to me that Peter too should be admired for his ability to comprehend what others were missing.

I think I've always been slow to come to the same realisation about the miraculous, and still struggle to have the ready faith that Peter displays. I know that I'm not alone in that though, which is the reason that Becky and I wanted to write this book, sharing something of our own stories by way of illustration. In *Growing in Circles*, I've already described something of my journey of faith, including an encounter with God that happened during my time as a student.[4] I was already active in mission and evangelism, but desperate to see more fruit. With a student outreach team, we were holding weekly Bible studies with foreign students as a way of sharing our faith, but no one ever became a believer. As a result, there was a growing cry in my heart for more. What happened was that, over the course of about a week, each time I laid down to sleep I began to experience a great sense of God being present with me. I remember being filled with a sense of joy and peace, not wanting the moment to end. Looking back now, I know that it was a healing experience, enabling my heart to catch up with what I believed in my head. And, without doing anything different, there was a marked change in the fruit that came from those Bible studies.

What I gained from that series of encounters – a deeper experience of God, and perhaps an increased anointing – resulted in my becoming much more open to the supernatural. I started to read the Bible in a new light, seeing what was possible, rather than thinking that what was recorded on the pages of Scripture was exceptional, only for that time, so that we would believe in Jesus but shouldn't expect him to be at work the same way today. Encountering his power and presence made me realise that he is just as active as he ever was! So, I quickly moved to a theologically charismatic perspective, with a heightened expectation of God's intervention and involvement in the everyday, even though I was still not experiencing much of it. I began to wonder: *was there a barrier?* Surely, if he is *"the same yesterday, today and forever"* (Hebrews 13:8), then what I had glimpsed must be always true? How could I see more? Or, what I now realise was a more pertinent question, *what was stopping me from seeing?* For me, the answer was closely connected to my rational and analytical outlook.

Reading the Bible has been very important to me throughout my Christian life. It was through reading it myself for the first time that I really met Jesus, understood what he'd done for me on the cross, and begun to get a sense of the big story into which God calls us. I have always delighted in both the beauty of what the Bible reveals and its power to explain our experience of life, and so I've regularly memorised verses or passages which have spoken to me. One of the first Bible verses that I memorised was Proverbs 3:5-6: *"Trust in the LORD with all your heart and lean not on your own understanding; in all your ways submit to him, and he will make your paths straight."*

Most people love those verses because they find comfort in the promise of God's guidance. I've come to see another equally important truth there – namely that the opposite of *"trust"* is *"leaning on your own understanding"*. Leaning on our own understanding actually blocks our ability to receive by faith, and makes it harder for God to lead us into new things. For me, as someone who is by nature very rational, logical and scientific in my approach to life, that indicates a huge potential issue. In the Christian life, often our greatest dangers come when our strengths are pushed too far. A strong analytical mind has been a great blessing to me in many aspects of my life. It has enabled me to think clearly, to dive down into a more accurate understanding so that I can explain things to others, to plan strategically and break big projects down into smaller steps so that we can get started on big visions without being quite as overwhelmed. I thank God for those strengths and for how he uses them in my life.

But I am also aware that, apart from his gracious intervention in my life, I would easily be someone who would only believe in what he could explain scientifically. I could quite easily be a thorough-going materialist, believing only in what I could see. The whole "science versus faith" debate is, in many expressions, no debate at all. Most often, science seeks to explain the "how", whereas faith seeks the "who" and "why" behind the process. As a student, I was a mathematician, eventually studying fairly obscure things like cosmology.[5] I think that, because of my experience of God, what might have undermined faith for some people, simply served to enlarge my faith – after all, the more that we understand, the more we realise how much there still remains to be understood. More than that, I came away from my studies not only aware of the extent of our ignorance, but also convinced that what we do already know points to a good, guiding Creator. Despite the danger of sounding an over-simplification, I would nevertheless say that the universe is simply too finely balanced to have occurred by accident.

The rational mind is a gift from God, but it needs to be disciplined so that it doesn't become too arrogant and believe that everything can be comprehended. Many of the basic tenets of faith warn against that prideful assumption. *"As the heavens are higher than the earth, so my ways are higher than your ways, and my thoughts than your thoughts"* (Isaiah 55:9). *"We walk by faith, not by sight"* (2 Corinthians 5:7). In other words, we can't simply go by what we see (or understand). God exists and is beyond our understanding. He invites us to seek understanding, because that is an important part of "knowing" and central to a healthy relationship, but cautions us not to imagine that we will ever come to a position where we can comprehend him completely.

If God exists and interacts, which was what I had experienced, then the supernatural should be expected, at least from time to time. As it says in Hebrews 11:6, *"Without faith it is impossible to please God because anyone who comes to him must believe that he exists and that he rewards those who earnestly seek him."*

In other words, the Father wants all of his children not only to believe that he exists, but also that his goodness finds tangible expression in our experience and, through us, in the experience of others. We should expect to see the inbreaking of his Kingdom. It actually makes rational sense.

More than that, God steps into our experience to invite us into relationship with him. Miracles help us believe. Jesus performed signs and wonders so that the crowds would understand the goodness of God and put their faith in him. The point of "signs and wonders" is that they reveal something. "Signs" point to something that you can't see until you make the journey. "Wonders" exist to make us wonder, or in other words, to think and to change our mind about what we consider to be "reality". We're not allowed to demand signs in order to believe, as the Pharisees did when they didn't like the miracles that he *had* been doing (Matthew 16:1). Jesus refused to perform signs for them, just as he had refused to perform for Satan during his temptation in the wilderness (Matthew 4:7).

However, God loves to intervene to help those who are genuinely open to believing. Jesus himself said that the point of miracles is to help us to believe: *"Believe me when I say that I am in the Father and the Father is in me; or at least believe on the evidence of the works themselves"* (John 14:11).And the Apostle John, who is more selective in his recording of miracles than any of the other gospel writers, makes the point that those that he did include are there for one reason only: *"Jesus performed many other signs in the presence of his disciples, which are not recorded in this book. But these are written that you may believe that Jesus is the Messiah, the Son of God, and that believing you may have life in his name"* (John 20:31). Experience matters.

Experiencing God is a factor in the growth of all Christians, and specifically if we are to be fruitful. On my shelf for many years has been a book that I bought from a second-hand shop in Cambridge when a student, called *Deeper Experiences of Famous Christians*.[6] It had a profound effect on me, but I hadn't come across it again since. It was only when I was doing some work for this book that I discovered that Dallas Willard referred to it as, "the one book other than the Bible that has most influenced me." In an article he said,

"I had been raised in religious circles of very fine people where the emphasis had been exclusively on faithfulness to right beliefs, and upon bringing others to profess those beliefs. Now that, of course, is of central importance. But when that alone is emphasised, the result is a dry and powerless religious life, no matter how sincere, and one constantly vulnerable to temptations of all kinds.

Therefore, to see actual invasions of human life by the presence and action of God, right up into the twentieth century, greatly encouraged me to believe that the life and promises given in the person of Christ and in Scripture were meant for us today. I saw that ordinary individuals who sought the Lord would find him real – actually, that he would come to them and convey his reality. It was clear that these 'famous Christians' were not seeking experiences, not even experiences of the filling or baptism of the Spirit. They were seeking the Lord, his Kingdom and his holiness. (Matthew 6:33)."[7]

Although the book focuses on people who were mightily used by God – heroes of the faith such as John Wesley, George Müller, William and Catherine Booth – what I took from it was that they were all people who *went on* to be mightily used by God. In other words, their experience of God's presence and power was the cause, not the result, of their remarkable lives. The more biographies that I read, the more I found the link between being filled by God and being used by God. Even people not normally known as charismatics – such as Billy Graham – often turned out to have had what I would understand as a "charismatic experience" of the Holy Spirit.[8]

Experience matters. On the day of Pentecost, recorded for us in Acts 2, the crowds witnessed something that they didn't understand. As ever, there was the usual mixture of responses – the same responses of fear, misunderstanding and misattribution that the disciples displayed when they first saw a figure walking on the water. In Acts 2, some attributed the behaviour of the disciples to alcohol and made fun of them. Others sensed, from the miraculous sign of them all being able to understand what was being said in their own language, that this was indeed of God. They asked two great questions, which shows that they were ready to receive something new from God. *"What does this mean?"* (Acts 2:12) and *"What should we do?"* (Acts 2:37). Actually, I've come to see that these two questions are at the heart of Jesus' call for us to *"repent and believe the gospel"* (Mark 1:15). "Repent" in Greek means "change your worldview or mindset" and "believe" carries the sense of "trusting and acting accordingly" (i.e. more than mere intellectual assent). Peter was the ideal man to answer both questions! What he had experienced had shaped both how he now saw the world and how he acted within it.

"Lean not on your own understanding" (Proverbs 3:5) doesn't mean that we shouldn't seek to understand. Far from it: *"The Lord looks down from heaven on all mankind to see if there are any who understand, any who seek God"* (Psalm 14:2). We are meant to apply our minds to the worthiest possible subject of our contemplation, God himself, but never to think that we could fully comprehend. He is not a subject to be mastered, but someone to be adored. And, in loving him, rather than merely seeking to intellectually appreciate him, the paradox is that he will become even more wonderful to both heart and mind.

Endnotes

1. http://www.guinnessworldrecords.com/news/2012/5/sherlock-holmes-awarded-title-for-most-portrayed-literary-human-character-in-film-tv-41743/. Note, however, that Sherlock is the most portrayed human character, not the overall most portrayed literary character in film. That title belongs to Dracula, who has been portrayed in 272 films.

What that says about us as a race, I'm not sure!

2. Matthew 14:28.

3. This phrase occurs many times in the Sherlock Holmes stories, e.g. *The Sign of Four*, p92, The Penguin Complete Sherlock Holmes (1981).

4. p17.

5. I actually sat in lectures given by Stephen Hawking, which eventually became his bestselling book, *A Brief History of Time*. Like many then and since, I didn't understand a word of it ... way above my abilities.

6. *Deeper Experiences of Famous Christians* by James G. Lawson (1911), now available online as a scanned copy on books.google.com.

7. *Published in Indelible Ink: 22 Prominent Christian Leaders Discuss the Books That Shape Their Faith*, edited by Scott Larsen, WaterBrook Press (2003).

8. http://daibach-welldigger.blogspot.co.uk/2012/03/billy-graham-encounters-holy-spirit-in.html.

Chapter 3
Taught by the Spirit

It can be a fun but imprecise activity to try to assess the personality types of people in the Bible, but if I had to stick my neck out and name a Bible character who might favour the more "left brain" (rational) approach to life, perhaps my namesake, the Apostle Paul, might be a good candidate. He seems, from his writings especially, to be very at home in the language of logic, principles and propositions. Remember though, that this is a man who *was caught up into paradise*, *heard inexpressible things* and had *surpassingly great revelations* (2 Corinthians 12:4,7). Paul's earlier life, characterised by zeal for the truth and a sense of his own rightness, tragically led him not to love God but to persecute Christians. Only when he encountered Jesus, in a very tangible way, did he realise how wrong he had been and how much he had to learn.

I've wondered also whether we can see through Paul's

life an increasing awareness of the need for supernatural demonstrations of power to back up his preaching. Immediately after his conversion, Paul (still called Saul at that point), began to preach, both fearlessly and effectively. Some years later, Barnabas brought him to Antioch to help teach the new Gentile believers (Acts 11:19-26). No doubt, whilst there, he saw signs and wonders – probably implied by phrases such as *"the Lord's hand was with them"* (verse 21) and *"evidence of the grace of God"* (verse 23) – but there are no references to Paul personally performing miracles in Jesus' name until we get to his first missionary journey, recounted in Acts 13.

I wrote in *Growing in Circles* about how significant I see his encounter with the false prophet Elymas to be[1], and it does seem that, from that time, supernatural signs accompany Paul's preaching, e.g. Acts 14:3: *"Paul and Barnabas spent considerable time there, speaking boldly for the Lord, who confirmed the message of his grace by enabling them to do miraculous signs and wonders."* Reading into the following chapters though, I can see a further turning point between Acts 17 and Acts 18.

Paul's preaching in Athens (Acts 17:16-33) is often held up as a model of how we should preach in the modern world. In the context of idolatry and competing philosophies, Paul delivers an erudite and winsome sermon, in which he carefully constructs his argument, building bridges from common ground and quoting their own poets and writers.

However, as soon as Jesus' resurrection is mentioned, everything seems to come to a crashing halt. It says that *"some sneered"*, others were merely interested and wanted to hear more on another occasion, and *"a few became followers of Paul and believed"* (verse 34). Of all the incidents of gospel preaching in Acts, this does not stand out as especially effective in terms of lives changed.

After that, however, Paul left Athens and went to Corinth. What is recorded in Acts 18 of his ministry in Corinth indicates that it was an extremely tough time, but *"many"* Corinthians *"believed and were baptised"* (Acts 18:8). More significantly, we have two epistles to *"the church in Corinth"* but nothing to *"the church in Athens"*. There appears not to have been a significant Christian presence in Athens during the first century, despite it being such an important city.

What was the difference between the two cities? Perhaps part of the answer lies in Paul's approach. In 1 Corinthians 2:1-5, Paul writes, *"When I came to you, brothers, I did not come with eloquence or superior wisdom"* (i.e. as he had preached in Athens), *"...for I resolved to know nothing while I was with you except Jesus Christ and him crucified ... My message and my preaching were not with wise and persuasive words, but with a demonstration of the Spirit's power, so that your faith might not rest on men's wisdom, but on God's power."* This isn't an anti-intellectual comment, as some have seen it, but rather a statement of the need for the supernatural in evangelism. Paul, I believe, had increasingly seen the weakness of trying to argue people into the Kingdom, and was realising that what persuaded people was an encounter with God.

Partnership with the Spirit of God is the heart of discipleship. In his second letter to the Corinthians, Paul reminds them of his ministry there by saying, *"The things that mark an apostle – signs, wonders and miracles – were done among you with great perseverance"* (2 Corinthians 12:12). And, after his work in Corinth, Paul's next focus was Ephesus, where Acts 19 records that, *"God did extraordinary miracles through Paul"* (verse 11). Far from being purely a *"preacher of the word"*, he knew that his preaching could easily become self-reliance if he didn't expect and make space for the supernatural inbreaking of God to confirm his word. Paul embraced that, and so should we. We should always be looking for that "something more" to accompany what we do, so that people see God working through us. Otherwise there's a danger that we rely on natural gifts and learned skills. If we are truly partners with God, the way that we serve him will reveal that we are expectant: seeking his leading, asking for his wisdom, and trusting in his power. We are merely following the pattern that Jesus set in his three-year earthly ministry – "words" and "works" together revealing the Kingdom.

In Psalm 16:11, David wrote, *"You make known to me the path of life; you will fill me with joy in your presence, with eternal pleasures at your right hand."* The *"path of life"* here is explained by words that encompass both intimacy (his presence) and authority (being at his right hand, which signifies honour and stewardship). Growing into this relationship is to be our life's work, but fortunately we have a teacher. In 1 Corinthians 2, after speaking about his reliance on supernatural signs, Paul goes on to speak about the role of the Holy Spirit, who both reveals (verses 6-10) and teaches (verses 11-16). The key thing is that the Spirit works so that *"we may understand what God has freely given us"* (verse 12). He reveals what is already ours, and teaches us how to inhabit it. We are to become Spirit-people in word, and (as we'll see) in deeds too. In my own experience, being filled with the Spirit is just the beginning. The Spirit has a personality, he is not simply a "power". Once we know that he resides within us, we are ready to be taught by the Spirit.

Learning to walk in partnership with God has been one of the most fulfilling aspects of my spiritual journey. As a student, leading the International Student Outreach Team was a proving ground for me. Not only was I learning how to share my faith with others, I was also learning to lead a team of peers. It wasn't long before I felt that this was how I was meant to spend my life. I offered myself as a candidate to be ordained, even though I'd never really met any clergy who shared my background or culture. Of course, there are plenty of ordained people who come from all types of backgrounds, just not that many in Cambridge in those days. Having had a very varied experience of different churchmanships helped, and meant that I somehow sailed through the process and was accepted for training at the rather young age of 20. I had already committed to continuing the overseas student ministry for a year after graduation, so it was 1989 when I arrived at Wycliffe Hall theological college in Oxford to train.

Wycliffe was where I learnt to take my first practical steps into the supernatural. There is a difference between having experiences and being able to walk in the light of them. Theologians distinguish between "theory" (how we understand, in this case "theology") and "praxis" (how we live out our beliefs). Many people have some experience of God that has opened them up to new perspectives and insights, but without a practical model they don't know what to do with what they've been given. For example, you may have seen God heal, but if you don't know a good model of how to pray for someone then it will most likely leave your Christian faith unchanged for all practical purposes.

In 1989, the same year I arrived at Wycliffe, New Wine was in its infancy. That summer had seen the first New Wine summer conference week at Shepton Mallet, bringing together people who wanted to learn more about ministering in the power of the Holy Spirit. The conference was David Pytches' way of responding to the growing number of leaders who wanted to introduce the renewal into their churches, but needed their people to see demonstrated what was being taught so that it wasn't just theory. The root of all that New Wine has become lies in the visit of John Wimber to Saint Andrew's Chorleywood over the Pentecost weekend of 1981. What Wimber brought was not only a balanced, biblical theology of the Kingdom (that it is both now here and not yet fully here), but crucially also a praxis – practical teaching about how to live out what the Bible tells us about Kingdom ministry. Just as Jesus demonstrated the nature of the Kingdom by performing signs, wonders and miracles, so Wimber taught (and modelled) an expectation that God would back up what was preached with works of power. The power of that weekend visit was remarkable, and as David Pytches and the church continued to learn and grow in what they'd received, giving it away to all who wanted it, something began that continues to this day.

But, arriving at college in 1989, this was all still reasonably new. I had not come into contact with charismatics before and the renewal was considered controversial. There were, however, a few students at Wycliffe who were committed charismatics. One was my friend, John Peters, who was to give me the praxis to go with the theology to which my experience of the Spirit was leading me.

It's fair to say that I struggled at first to fit into Wycliffe Hall. I was new to evangelical circles and felt culturally at odds with most of my fellow students. I hadn't attended the same schools, or the same churches or camps, and to top it off, I had long hair. The place where I found my confidence was in the college football team. Wycliffe, as a "permanent private hall" in the University, was essentially a graduate college, so most of the teams that we played in the Oxford leagues were significantly younger, comprised of 18-21 year olds, who would turn up smoking and drinking yet still manage to run around like greyhounds! By contrast, the Wycliffe team was, on average, ten years older. What we lacked in speed and fitness, we could only make up in brawn and commitment. This resulted in some rather feisty games, where the undergraduates turned up expecting an easy game against the "trainee vicars" (well, you would, wouldn't you?) and discovered that they were playing full-grown men who knew that, if they didn't stop you first time, they would never catch you afterwards.. It has to be said that, not unsurprisingly, the Wycliffe team was therefore known for being fairly physical. The result was that the person that the undergraduates usually targeted for retaliation was the long-haired centre-forward who was roughly their own age and build. In that first term, I came off the field each week battered and bruised, and rarely in a state to play again soon. I would limp back into the Common Room and collapse into an armchair.

But each week, other students would pray for me to be healed. They began to model for me how to pray for the sick, and despite my injuries being trivial and not in any way life-threatening, each week I experienced healing. Having played a lot of football, I knew that my subsequent recovery was not natural, and often it was instantaneous. Although

I wondered at the theological issues that were raised by the healing of my trivial injuries, when compared to those far worthier of healing, I couldn't deny the reality of what happened when I received prayer.

John saw this and, ever the evangelist, started to ask me what I believed about the Spirit and where I stood. Early on, he asked me whether I spoke in tongues (the spiritual gift mentioned in the New Testament, whereby we speak in languages that we haven't learned). Really, the only teaching that I had come across about tongues had been that the gift of tongues was divisive, and probably unnecessary. I told him that I'd heard about tongues and had actually prayed to receive the gift but hadn't experienced anything.

During that week of experiencing the filling of Spirit as I waited for sleep, I had prayed that God would give me this "odd gift" that I'd heard about, but nothing had happened. I'd tried to speak a few syllables, but had quickly decided that what was coming out was "just me". In his usual sensitive manner, John replied, "Of course it's you, but it's not just you – Acts 2 says that *'they spoke in tongues, as the Spirit enabled them'*" (Acts 2:4).

There's a partnership – we mustn't expect anything to emerge from our mouths unless we decide to make sounds. Neither should we expect that a language will emerge fully-formed. These were new thoughts to me and, frankly, I wasn't convinced! John insisted on praying for me to receive the gift though, speaking in tongues himself and encouraging me to join in. I managed a few syllables, gradually becoming more fluent and confident and was assured, "That's it!"

He left me with instruction to practise the new language for five minutes a day, and an invitation to accompany him on the following evening and act as his "ministry team" for a talk in a nearby undergraduate college.

When we turned up at that college Christian Union event, there were maybe thirty students present. John spoke about the power of the Holy Spirit in evangelism and then offered to pray for them. Actually, if I recall correctly, he didn't give them an option! We put a cassette tape of worship music on in the background (this was a while ago, when cassette tapes were all we had!) and proceeded to invite the Spirit to come. My instructions were to "watch where God was moving and go and pray for anyone where you see God touching them."

The only problem was that I had no idea what the signs of God touching someone were! Quickly, John was praying for one person, then another, then another – rapidly running out of limbs to lay on people – whilst I stood there unsure of what to do. I remember him gesturing with his head (about the only option he had left for pointing) towards one girl, obviously suggesting that it might be nice if I got involved and prayed for someone. As I looked, I could see that she did seem to be responding in a slightly different way to others around her – a very intent look on her face and swaying slightly – so I went over to add my massive faith to hers, trying to look like I knew what I was doing.

Praying for her did seem to increase the magnitude of whatever was going on, but I had no idea what to pray. What I remembered though was that John had said, "If you run out of prayers, use that new gift of tongues that you don't believe in!" So, I reasoned, "I've got nothing to lose; no one can hear me over the music, so I might as well."

The moment I started to speak in tongues, quietly under my breath so no one could hear me doing something that felt ridiculous, she fell to the floor and proceeded to flop like a fish. No one was more surprised than me, but I thought I'd better follow her down and pray for her, again trying to give the impression that I knew what I was doing! (It may be a faulty memory, but I'm pretty certain that at that point John caught my eye and gave me the thumbs up). She carried on with the flopping motions for about ten minutes, before she gradually relaxed and sat up. When she'd caught her breath, she explained something of what she'd been experiencing.

When she had been much younger, her father had tried to teach her to swim. However, his way of doing that had been to throw her into the deep end and only pull her out when she was clearly not keeping her head above water. Despite her tears, he'd proceeded to do this repeatedly. Not surprisingly, she'd never felt able to fully trust her father from that day and had a deeply impaired relationship with him. In actual fact, that impairment had carried over into her relationship with her Heavenly Father as well. She had become guarded and found it hard to trust. During the prayer time though, she had gradually begun to relive that experience, except that this time, she was aware of the presence of Jesus in the water with her, holding her and bearing her up. Something in the encounter that she had with the Lord delivered her from a deep-seated and life-controlling fear. She went off to phone her father, initiating contact for the first time in years. I met her about a year later and her relationships, with both her earthly and her heavenly father, were transformed. That experience was a great blessing for her, but it was also a great gift to me. When you see someone's life changed so dramatically, in such a short space of time, then you'll always want to see God's ministry rather than your own. What was so powerful for me was seeing God use something that I couldn't understand cognitively; instead I simply had to trust him. That posture is the foundation of being able to move in spiritual gifts.

I think, for that reason, the gift of tongues is a "gateway gift" for many people. With most other spiritual gifts, our part in the partnership is more obvious – we are more involved in crafting the form of the prayer, word, act or whatever. With tongues, all we contribute is the decision whether to open our mouths and make sounds or not! In fact, that's Paul's point when he says, *"If I pray in a tongue, my spirit prays, but my mind is unfruitful"* (1 Corinthians 14:14). Speaking in tongues is helpful (we "edify ourselves", verse 4) but not intelligible (unless interpreted). God therefore wants us to practise what we don't understand (speaking in tongues), but also to pray "with our understanding" (verse 15), especially when we're in the presence of others.

This is not the place to explore in detail the gift of tongues – I recommend instead the chapter in John Peters' book, *Third Person*[2] – save to say that I believe that it is a gift available to all believers. No one has to speak in tongues to demonstrate their spiritual maturity, but all of us potentially can.[3] Paul knew the power of this gift, even though he couldn't fully understand it – *"I thank God that I speak in tongues more than all of you"* (1 Corinthians 14:18).

The spiritual gifts are just that, *gifts* given by God that need to be used in partnership with him. Even when they might overlap with natural talents, such as a teaching gift, they require a spiritual understanding and approach. The important thing is that we recognise that all believers are called to actively pursue their use. If you like, we need an experience of them, and theology for them, and a praxis (practical wisdom of how to use them).

"Now about gifts of the Spirit, brothers and sisters, I do not want you to be uninformed" (1 Corinthians 12:1), Paul wrote, which sadly remains the case for much of the Church today. It is often pointed out that at the heart of Paul's discussion about spiritual gifts is chapter 13 – one of the most wonderful chapters in the Bible about love. What we mustn't conclude though, is that pursuing love (the greatest thing) allows us to neglect the pursuit of power or partnership with God. The verse immediately following that great chapter is this:

"Follow the way of love and eagerly desire gifts of the Spirit, especially prophecy" (1 Corinthians 14:1). If we really desire to love others, we will seek to do so in a way that enables them to encounter God. As it says in 1 Corinthians 12:7, *"to each one the manifestation of the Spirit is given for the common good."* "Manifestation" means "that which makes visible, tangible, obvious". We are all equipped by God to make him real in the experience of others, for their benefit not our own. Truly loving others will lead us to want to be able to speak to them his words, or have them experience his love, not merely ours.

Setting love in the middle of the chapters on spiritual gifts says something very important about the motivation and manner that we need in this pursuit, but we mustn't miss the challenge of seeking to move with God in this supernatural ministry. What chapters 12 and 14 have in common is that they require us to express spiritual hunger and adopt the humble posture of a learner. Another danger of venerating understanding, though, is the false belief that we need to completely understand before we practise these gifts. Hunger and humility don't always come easily, but they are vital if we are to better learn how to hear God's voice, pray effectively for others, or exercise any of the other spiritual gifts.[4] God's classroom is the world; the Holy Spirit teaches us "on the job" because, ultimately, the gifts are for mission, revealing God to others.

No one likes to be seen making mistakes, and learning

to do anything new inevitably includes trying and failing. You don't have to have a problem with perfectionism to be nervous about the thought of stepping out in dependence on God. However difficult, though, you have to learn to trust God. He will do what he has promised and he seems to love it when we take him at his word. In training people to use the spiritual gifts, we've often used the phrase "be naturally supernatural" to describe how to minister to others. This means that bizarre behaviours and super-spiritual performances simply divert the focus away from God, and may actually make it harder for people to receive. We stand by that. The downside of the phrase, though, as Alan Scott pointed out at the New Wine summer conference in 2015, is that none of us feel that it's "natural" to step into the supernatural at first! His advice is wonderful: just be "awkwardly supernatural", until you become more familiar with the gifts and moving in them becomes more natural with time and experience.

Jesus promised that *"whoever believes in me will do the things that I have been doing, and they will do even greater things than these"* (John 14:12).[5] It's no surprise to me that he immediately goes on to talk about the ministry of the Holy Spirit, specifically that he will *"teach you all things"* (John 14:26). If we step out, then of course growth is possible. After all, we have a great Teacher.

Endnotes

1. *Growing in Circles*, chapter 6 – Authority Leads to Destiny. In this chapter I note that the occasion of his name-change from Saul to Paul comes when he is first recorded as taking up his authority in a clearly supernatural context. This is also the incident which signals the change of leadership within the apostolic team, from "Barnabas and Saul" to "Paul and Barnabas".

2. Especially the commentary on 1 Corinthians that appears in chapter 9 of *Third Person* by John Peters (New Wine/River Publishing 2017)

3. In this interpretation I follow Gordon Fee (*The First Epistle to the Corinthians*, New International Commentary on the New Testament, Eerdmans 1987). The discussion of spiritual gifts (chapters 12-14) is actually part of a wider unit beginning at chapter 11, where the subject is what we do when we come together for worship. The point being made is not that only some people have certain gifts, but rather that we shouldn't all expect to use the same ones when we gather.

4. For further study on the gifts of the Holy Spirit, I recommend the following books:

   Learning to Heal, John Coles (Authentic Media, 2010)
   Learning to Hear God's Voice, Mark Aldridge (New Wine, 2016)
   Everyday Supernatural: Living a Spirit-Led Life without Being Weird,
   Mike Pilavachi and Andy Croft (David C Cook, 2016)

5. I've written more about this in chapter 2 of *Growing in Circles*.

Chapter 4
Learning to Let Go

One common, but very misleading, phrase is "blind faith". But *"we walk by faith, not by sight"*[1] shouldn't be taken to mean that faith is blind! There's an old joke that reminds us that we don't only use one sense:

Two men dressed in pilots' uniforms walk up the aisle of the aircraft. Both are wearing dark glasses, one is using a guide dog, and the other is tapping his way along the aisle with a cane. Nervous laughter spreads through the cabin, but the men enter the cockpit, the door closes, and the engines start up. The passengers begin glancing nervously around, searching for some kind of sign that this is just a little practical joke. None is forthcoming. The plane moves faster and faster down the runway, and the people sitting in the window seats realise they're headed straight for the water at the edge of the airport property. Just as it begins to look as though the plane will plow straight into the water, panicked screams fill the cabin. At that moment, the plane lifts smoothly into the air. The passengers relax and laugh a little sheepishly, and soon all retreat into their magazines and books, secure in the knowledge that the plane is in good hands. Meanwhile, in the cockpit, one of the blind pilots turns to the other and says, "You know, Bob, one of these days, they're going to scream too late and we're all going to die!"

Some would have us think that "walking by faith" is just as risky a prospect as being in a plane piloted by blind pilots! However, the opposite of sight isn't blindness; often it's faith which sees something that is invisible.

Anyone who has been in a group environment – whether at school, in a youth group, or increasingly in professional environments – will be familiar with "trust exercises". These are team building activities that are intended to create mutual empathy and a sense of being able to rely upon each other, as well as developing communication amongst the group. One of the classic trust building exercises is falling backwards into the arms of someone else who catches you before you hit the ground. Many people find it hard, even though the reality is that a tiny percentage of people ever end up on the floor! Our hesitation stems from a lack of confidence that someone, who perhaps we don't know well, is alert to the situation, willing to catch us, and able to bear our weight. That struggle to let go and trust someone else is analogous to our struggle to let go and trust God. This is despite repeated assurances in the Bible that his eyes are constantly upon us, that he is faithful, and that he is able. It's therefore important that we learn to listen attentively to testimonies – those who have stepped out and trusted him always report that he is trustworthy; those who take risks of faith don't always get everything right, but they rarely regret it.

Being trusting is spiritually healthy. It's only living in a broken world, where not everyone and everything is trustworthy, that qualifies that statement. Our natural response to bad, or even normal, experiences of that brokenness is to develop the need to retain control. Those control issues are usually rooted in one of two problems – pride or fear. We either judge others as not being able to do things as well as us, or we fear that they won't do them with our best interests at heart. This shows that what we need isn't *control*, but a sense that *someone suitable is in control*. Children aren't born with control issues – they are happy to trust in the competence and goodwill of their carers. (This partly explains why some people spend their whole life seeking the security of parent-figures). As we mature, we become independent of our parents and take personal responsibility. What we often fail to do, though, is to develop an appropriate dependence on our Heavenly Father, who is always faithful and able.

I wouldn't say that I'm a control freak, but I have been known to take things from Becky's hands when they're not working, such as her phone if it's playing up. I might even say, "Here, let me have a look at that for you," but it's often after I've already taken it! And if I was completely honest with myself, in many situations in life my underlying belief would be, "I think I know how to do this, so we ought to do it my way." That isn't always true and it's certainly not any reflection on Becky or the other people around me, and can leave people offended.

Clearly it becomes even more of a problem when it affects my spiritual life. I wonder if that's what broke in Peter when he, the professional fisherman, saw the catch of fish that resulted from following Jesus' instructions (Luke 5). Things go better when we let God take control. The process of surrendering control to God is not an easy one though, because it addresses deep issues in us. That was certainly the case for me.

One of my most profound experiences of surrendering to God came towards the end of my first curacy. I had been ordained for a couple of years, and it was agreed that I would remain back on the Wirral, where we lived, in charge of the church whilst the vicar, the other curate and many church members went to the New Wine summer conference. This was 1994, and when they returned from that week away, the group came back having been powerfully touched by an extraordinary move of the Spirit. In time, this season came to be known as the "Toronto Blessing", having originated from a small church on the edge of Toronto Airport. Since the January of that year, that church had hosted nightly meetings in which people were so affected that hundreds fell to the floor, were overcome with laughter or tears, and even, in some cases, made noises like animals. Not surprisingly, the manifestations that people experienced proved to be highly controversial and, in reports of what was happening, often distracted attention from the deep things that God was doing.

Manifestations of the Spirit are nothing new, having precedent in the Bible as well as in revivals throughout Christian history. Essentially, they are the results of our body's response to deep stimuli. It makes sense that when we are touched at a deep emotional level, there will be a physical response. This is the underlying theory of polygraphs, commonly known as lie detectors. The emotions that we experience cannot be completely hidden, always affecting us physically. We ought therefore to expect that when God deeply touches people, there will in many cases be an outward expression as a result.

The form of the manifestation often has some connection with what the person is experiencing – e.g. shaking may occur as they receive more of God's power – but not always, and the significance is only ever in the fruit of what happens. We need discernment to get a sense of what God might be doing and ultimately all that matters is the fruit that it bears in their lives. As we used to say when many people were falling in the presence of God, "It's not how they fall down that matters, but how they get up."

For some, that experience of God's presence was so overwhelming that they found themselves falling to the ground, so that, by choice or simply because they could do nothing else, their whole attention was focused on God.

The phenomenon of falling under God's power was a particular sticking point for me. Over my few years as a charismatic I'd often seen people respond in that manner, but when our church group came back from New Wine suddenly that became the case with many people who came forward for prayer in our services. For about a month, I saw people having very powerful encounters with God – even when I prayed for them, and even though I'd not been present at the conference to "catch a different anointing" or anything like that. I received prayer myself many times over those weeks but never felt that anything especially significant was happening.

To be honest, I began to feel a bit perplexed and wanted, if this was genuinely God, to make sure that I was part of it. I'd heard the phrase, "God will not give you what you can't handle", and it seemed to be a good interpretation of Luke 11:13: *"If you then, though you are evil, know how to give good gifts to your children, how much more will your Father in heaven give the Holy Spirit to those who ask him!"* God is good, and his Spirit is the best gift that we could ever receive. Listening to some teaching from Toronto about "surrendering control to God", I began to wonder whether my issue about "not falling over" expressed some reluctance to really let go. Over the years, when receiving prayer, I had, on occasion, felt unsteady – as if the weightiness of God's presence[2] was pressing me backwards. However, on each occasion I took a step back and steadied myself. My analytical and rational outlook led me too often to be an observer of what God was doing, when, as I came to realise, all he wanted me to be was a recipient.

Receiving prayer, I would often be conscious of what was going on around me, of other prayers being said near me, and certainly of my own body's reactions. Others might fall over, but I never did – and I never would. I once said that whenever I felt a gentle pressure forcing me backwards, that what I would be doing is calculating my angle of inclination and centre of gravity! (You must remember, I was a mathematician as a student...) As a result, I wouldn't fall over, I would take a step back. Then another. I jokingly said once that I've been marched from the front to the back of many churches during prayer ministry, one backward step at a time.

The truth, though, is that many people who fall over when prayed for do so because they can't be bothered to stand up any more; they just go with what God is doing. Falling (or not) had become a bit of a "hang up" for me. I wasn't willing to do anything that might simply be faking – surely people who fell had to have been "slain" in the Spirit, overcome by an overwhelming and irresistible power (as some clearly are) – but I ended up with my focus on my own reactions and actually resisting what God might have been doing.

The breakthrough came when I came to crisis point with the renewal in our church, determined to work out with God whether this was him or not. If it was genuine, why was I not experiencing the same power? I set apart an afternoon when Becky had gone to work and I would be alone in the house. Listening to recordings of John Arnott, the pastor of the Toronto church, about the need to surrender to God and let him do whatever he wanted, a thought suddenly occurred to me. "Why not cut out the middle-man?" If my hang-up was falling, why not start off lying down? That way I might not be as distracted by my body's reaction and posture. It seemed a reasonable experiment, so I finished listening to the teaching, put on some worship music, lay face up on the floor with a pillow under my head and prayed, "Lord, if this is of you, I want to experience it. I surrender all control to you. Come and fill me."

Nothing happened at first, but gradually I began to experience a greater sense of his presence. This increased, and kept increasing, until I felt full to the point of bursting. Right across my face, especially around my mouth, I felt a tingling, like "pins and needles" but not painful. I didn't understand what the phenomenon meant, but I knew that God had come. It was joyful, sweet and exhilarating.

In the middle of this experience, the phone rang. At that moment, I had a decision to make: I knew somehow that I could reassert control, get up and answer it. Instead I made one of the best decisions of my life, and decided to let the call go to the answerphone. I remained on the sitting room floor enjoying the presence of God.

Altogether, I think that the experience lasted perhaps thirty minutes. As I felt the Lord's touch subsiding, I slowly sat up and spent some time thanking him. I wasn't sure what it meant, or even what he had done, but I knew that he had met with me. I went to the answerphone and discovered that it was a message from a fellow curate, someone I knew from theological college and who had been ordained to serve in a church further north. His message was asking me what I thought about this strange thing that seemed to be gripping many in the Church. I called him back to say, "If you'd asked me an hour earlier, I would have said this, but after what has just happened my perspective has changed somewhat!"

Over the years, I've been prayed for publicly on countless occasions, and pray for God's presence to fill me on an almost daily basis in my personal prayers. The truth is that I rarely experience anything tangible. On a recent sabbatical, Becky and I visited Bethel Church, in Redding, California. It had been arranged that we would receive a special time of prophetic ministry. The words that were given were very helpful and confirmatory of many things that we knew the Lord was doing in us – but, as he delivered them, the man who was praying for me was having a great time! He was feeling every syllable and shaking under the power of what he was prophesying. Meanwhile, I was soaking it in, but outwardly, in terms of response, doing my regular impression of a brick. I occasionally feel the Lord's presence in a tangible manner, perhaps feeling that tingling around my mouth, but often nothing and I've learnt that it doesn't matter. Physical signs, even emotional reactions, really aren't essential. We receive by faith, and it's enough to take God at his word.

"How much more will the Father give the Holy Spirit to those who ask him", as Jesus said (Luke 11:13) – our part is simply demonstrating that hunger and asking. We can be confident that if we do our part, he will fulfil his promise. However, it would be a strange relationship where there was never an emotional component. And if it's emotional, because body, mind and spirit interpenetrate, then sometimes there may be a resulting physical sensation. Never having a tangible sense of his presence would be like never feeling emotion for the spouse you profess to love.

Letting go and surrendering control to God applies to far more than simply the realm of prayer ministry. If we are very "in control" people, as many of us with strong rational minds are, then we can easily take that approach into every area of our relationship with God. Whether it is praying for someone, or taking a journey of faith, we seriously limit what God can do if we don't make space for him to act in ways beyond our understanding. Trusting God's goodness relates both to allowing him to touch us and to lead us. Learning to do one has allowed me increasingly to do the other.

I had an object lesson in this when our church was embarking on a multi-million-pound building project about ten years ago. It was clear to everyone that we were going to have to have an incredibly successful capital campaign and raise a figure some ten times that which we had ever received as a church in giving during a single year. As someone with a maths background, the temptation naturally was to try and work out where the money was going to come from, thinking through the members of our church family and what I might be able to guess of their circumstances.

Fortunately, I never did that. In our own life, both Becky and I have never particularly struggled with believing that God would provide financially. We have seen him do great things for us, such as the time when we had uninsured medical bills in America and found ourselves £10,000 in debt on our first wedding anniversary. We found those debts completely paid off in months through the kindness of the Church on both sides of the Atlantic, even though most didn't know of our need.

I had always been careful in reconciling our accounts each month, but had felt the Lord challenge me not to trust so much in my own financial management, but to leave space for him to bless. That was my understanding of the curious passage in 1 Chronicles 21 where the Lord punishes David for taking a census of the fighting men. For twenty-five years, as a result, I haven't balanced a chequebook or planned a personal household budget (I don't recommend this). Generally, financial worries don't feature highly in our life: we try to live generously, aren't given to great extravagances, and just feel blessed in this area. That was much harder to embrace as an approach, and would have been wholly irresponsible, when it came time to lead our church into a capital campaign larger than anything we had ever done before.

At the time it was becoming clear to our team just how expensive and challenging the "CONNECT" project was going to be, I went with our Associate Minister, Simon, to a few days' residential training in Kingdom Ministry led by Bruce Collins. In one of the early sessions, Bruce spoke about prophetic ministry and its power to raise faith. Unbeknownst to us, he had asked one of his team, Freda Meadows, to be listening to the Lord for prophetic words for us as he spoke.

At the end of his talk, he asked her to share what the Lord had given her. Freda had several accurate words for others, but then turned to me. She had almost a whole page of notes which she proceeded to read out. Most of what was shared would have been instantly recognised as true of me to anyone who knew me (which she didn't). Right at the end though, Freda added, "Do you have any financial concerns?" Rather embarrassingly, I have to say that the church's challenge for some reason didn't even occur to me, so I said "no", on the basis of things being OK in our personal situation.

Fortunately, my colleague Simon was more alert and pointed out that we'd just been discussing the huge projected cost of the building works in the car on the way over! Freda then said, "Well, what I heard was the Lord saying to you, 'Don't worry about it, the money will come.'"

I realised immediately that this was a promise for our capital campaign. Over the coming years, the price of the project went up and up; there were many times when the financial shortfall was considerable and an incredible leadership challenge. There was always a temptation to leave faith out of the equation and calculate the finances myself, looking at it only from a human perspective. Of course, I regularly wished that the Lord would have given me another word or promise, but he didn't speak to me again about that aspect of the project for six years! I can honestly say though, that Freda's word sustained me and gave me confidence to keep leading the church forward. We eventually opened our new facilities in 2012, and what had become a £5million project was completely paid off by the end of that year. (You really shouldn't be impressed by me, but by those who believed that this was the Lord's will and were willing to be led on the strength of what I had sensed the Lord was saying...)

Whether it is submitting to being emotionally touched in a way that is more expressive than your norm, or being led by a prophetic sense into something where you can't easily see how it is going to work out, the challenge is to enlarge our comfort zone. Letting God do what he wants requires us to acknowledge the limitations of our own understanding and take adventures of risk on the basis of a firm belief in his goodness. We must learn how to walk by faith, "repenting and believing" the good news about God's kingdom (Mark 1:15) and how to live within it. Unless we're willing to look for God to lead and teach us, there will be a danger that our minds will limit our experience of his work, demanding that we understand before we enter in, or trying to follow Jesus as Lord whilst retaining control.

A strong, analytical, and rational mind is a gift from God. It can be a great strength, but we need to learn how to properly apply such a gift. If you relate strongly to these chapters, don't be discouraged. You have, in your mind, potentially a great ally. In 2 Corinthians 10, Paul talks about spiritual warfare in these terms: *"though we live in the world, we do not wage war as the world does. The weapons we fight with are not the weapons of the world. On the contrary, they have divine power to demolish strongholds. We demolish arguments and every pretension that sets itself up against the knowledge of God, and we take captive every thought to make it obedient to Christ"* (verse 3-5). Notice how much of an emphasis there is in this passage on our thought-lives: "arguments", "pretensions" and "thoughts". These strongholds stand against a true knowledge of God, and most spiritual warfare therefore happens between our ears.

It's ironic that those of us who value knowledge so much

can often, because of that approach, end up frustrated in our faith, as we come to realise that academic or theoretical knowledge about God is no substitute for personal knowledge of him. Rather than letting our minds be a barrier to spiritual growth, the best response is to co-opt the mind into the battle.

2 Timothy 1:7 says that, *"the Spirit God gave us does not make us timid, but gives us power, love and self-discipline"* (or "a sound mind" in some translations). But the original Greek word *sophronismos* comes from combining the word for mind (*phren*) with the word that is used throughout the New Testament for both "healing" and "salvation" (*sozo*). A "saved mind" is a strong weapon in spiritual warfare – we can use it to recall relevant truths from the Bible, think clearly about their implications, and have the mental discipline to act on what we know to be true. Our minds simply need to be surrendered to God, just as much as any other part of our lives. A "saved mind" is like a horse that has been "broken" – the process of getting a young horse to accept a rider. A broken horse is submitted – no less powerful, but now responsive to guidance.

The issue, according to the Apostle Paul, is where we allow our minds to be focused:

"Those who live according to the flesh have their minds set on what the flesh desires; but those who live in accordance with the Spirit have their minds set on what the Spirit

desires. The mind governed by the flesh is death, but the mind governed by the Spirit is life and peace. The mind governed by the flesh is hostile to God; it does not submit to God's law, nor can it do so. Those who are in the realm of the flesh cannot please God. You, however, are not in the realm of the flesh but are in the realm of the Spirit, if indeed the Spirit of God lives in you." (Romans 8:5-9)

If a strong mind is a gift that you've received from God, lay it back down at his feet and in his service. You may have done well in life through that blessing, succeeding in exams or getting on in the workplace, but it was given so that you might explore his kingdom, not build your own. We're all called to surrender everything to God, and to love him, *"with all your heart and with all your soul and with all your strength **and with all your mind**"* (Luke 10:27). As D.L. Moody was fond of saying, "Let God have your life; he can do more with it than you can."[3]

Endnotes

1. 2 Corinthians 5:7 (NKJV). The NIV translation has "live by faith", which is the plain sense of the verse, but the actual Greek word is that normally translated "walk".
2. It is often seen as significant that the Hebrew word for "glory" (*kabod*) can be literally translated as "weight" or "heaviness".
3. Quoted in *The Westminster Collection of Christian Quotations*, edited Martin Manser (Westminster John Knox, 2001).

"Heart Trouble"

What if Peter refused to step out of the boat because he was afraid or unable to take risks?

———

Becky's Story

Chapter 5
Lifting the Lid

"And we know that in all things God works for the good of those who love him, who have been called according to his purpose."
(Romans 8:28)

Thinking about barriers to the supernatural life is important, even vital, if we are at all serious about responding to the invitation of Jesus to "Come". It's an invitation extended to every one of us, every day, and if we don't deal with those things that hold us back from fully engaging in *"the good works prepared in advance of us to do"* (Ephesians 2:20) our experience of the Christian life will most likely be that it is dull, ineffective and unsatisfying to the point of frustration – instead of being the fulfilling, fruitful and healing adventure it was always meant to be.

For me, those barriers were high and seemed insurmountable for many years – and they were, as long as

I continued to try and make progress in my own strength. Because of the tragedies in my family history, I had what can be described in poetic language as a "wounded heart". Basically, difficult things had happened around and to me in my early life, so I learned to self-protect, be self-sufficient and self-contained, and I carried with me a heavy burden of guilt, disappointment and grief. Each of those contributed to the height of my barriers and made it impossible for me to respond willingly and wholeheartedly to Jesus' invitation to "Come" and join him in walking on the water. However, with God's constant presence and patience, my capitulation and surrender to begin with, and then my continuing determination to be free, my barriers have lowered and I'm more able to receive and respond to Jesus' "Come".

I had the privilege of growing up in a Christian home in the suburbs of St Louis, Missouri in America. My parents, from the state of Kansas, had both been committed Christians all their lives and by the time I came along, they were well established in a Southern Baptist Church, having moved to St Louis about three years previously. I had good teaching from both my parents and my church from my earliest days and as a result, asked God to live in my heart at the age of 4. In fact, I asked him repeatedly, night after night, for the next year or so, just to make sure. I'm very grateful to have had that grounding as a child and, as I said, it is a privilege to be raised in a Christian home, with a knowledge of God and to know from the start that he desired a relationship with me.

I was (and still am) a very sensitive person and as a child all my parents had to do was look at me sternly and I would start to cry. I had a very tender conscience and couldn't bear to be in trouble, or to cause any trouble. Partly that's my nature, partly that was a response to my family's situation. I was born into a family that had already experienced deep grief, and would experience more.

Today I have one older sister, Vicki, but if all my siblings had survived, there would be six of us instead of two. Vicki was my parents' first child, born before their first anniversary, but their second child, my brother Mike, died when he was eighteen months old. He had an epileptic seizure in the night, got twisted up and smothered in his blanket. My mother, who was only 20 at the time, found him dead in the morning when she went to get him up. This was, of course, heart-breaking for them as a young married couple so they decided to make a fresh start. They left California where my dad had gone for work and moved back to the Midwest for a job in St Louis.

My parents tried for another child and my mother had a still-birth in the fourth month of pregnancy, but the year after that I came along, happy and healthy. When I was two, they had another baby, my sister Rachel. All went well with her pregnancy and birth, but at six months, Rachel contracted bacterial meningitis and was very ill. She survived but was left severely brain damaged and unable to do anything for herself. My memories of Rachel are made up of her spending the day laying on the sofa, having to have everything done for her, and I mean everything, apart from swallow. Because I was a small child at the time, I was unaware of all my parents were coping with in caring for her. They were in and out of hospital as her heart would often stop, and she struggled with many other health complications. At the age of three, her body gave up completely and she died.

I was five at the time and came home from school with Vicki to find the house full of people. Our pastor was there and he sat us both down on his lap and told us that Rachel wasn't coming home again. Vicki, twelve by then, had a good grasp of what was going on. I was five and didn't really have a clue. However, as time went by, I got used to life without Rachel around, knowing she was in heaven with Jesus. As you would expect, things were not that straightforward for my parents by any means. They were grieving again and having to adjust after caring for a completely incapacitated child for three years.

Optimistically, they decided to try for another child one more time, and my sister Beth came along when I was seven. Beth developed epilepsy in her first year and was on heavy medication to control her seizures. Again, I was a child so didn't really grasp all that was going on. All I knew was that she had epilepsy and my parents were very stressed by how the medication affected her.

Five years passed, and by the time I was thirteen, my parents would often leave me to look after Beth for an hour or two when they needed to go out for a short time in the evenings. One particular evening, they wanted to visit a new couple who had attended church for the first time on Sunday and had come along to the group they led. While they were out, Beth was having her bath as usual, and I was playing the piano until it was time to get her out. She called to me and said she wanted to come out of the bath now. I called back and said I'd be there in a few minutes, as I wanted to finish the song I was playing. Unfortunately, by the time I did that and went to the bathroom, she had had a seizure and was floating face down in the water. I pulled her out and somehow managed to call 911. The paramedics came and took her to hospital. She was put on a ventilator for three days but then died.

After that day, the grief and guilt in our house were present in abundance. My parents felt guilty that they hadn't been there. They'd already had two children die and now they had to deal with losing a third – all that in addition to the pain of a stillbirth. (My dad has written about their experiences in a book called *Grace Enough for Three*[1]). I, of course, felt horribly guilty because I knew that if I had gone to get her out of the bath when she asked, she wouldn't have died.

It seems hard to believe now, with all the trauma and grief counselling available, but at the time, no one asked me what happened and no one asked me how I felt. My parents had so much to deal with themselves and I guess no one else felt it was their place – but that was fine with me! There was no way I wanted to talk about it and I just carried on with life on automatic pilot. I went back to school as if nothing had happened. I shoved the experience down, covered it up and forgot about it.

Except, of course, I didn't really forget about it. We all have experiences that wound us spiritually and emotionally and we would prefer to pretend those wounds aren't there, but that does not stop them influencing us in our everyday lives. This was a significant wound for me, and just because I wanted to detach myself from it and pretend it didn't happen, that doesn't mean it didn't affect me. When we do that, it's like putting a rubbish bin in the corner of our souls, shoving what we don't want to deal with into it and putting the lid on tight. Over time, if we don't invite Jesus to come in and deal with what we've put in there, it will start to stink, causing us problems and stopping us from being all God intends us to be.

I knew, all through my teenage years, that God wanted to help me with the trauma and guilt I felt, but I was very resistant. There were times in worship or quiet moments when thoughts would start to surface, but I would push them straight back down. I had no interest in taking the lid off my smelly bin, as it was just too painful to deal with. My faith in God was still strong, but I was stuck in guilt and not moving on.

My healing in this area is completely down to God's goodness. As I said, all through my teenage years, God was trying to get me to deal with my guilt over my sister's death, but I didn't want to. It wasn't until I came to study in Oxford in 1990 that I opened up to him and began the healing journey.

It was in January that year that I left home for England. My university in the US had a program that meant students could go to Oxford for a term or a year and study with tutors there. I decided to take advantage of this opportunity for a term in my final year before graduating. Randomly (if you don't take God into account), I was assigned to live in a place called Wycliffe Hall, a training college for Anglican ordinands. All my friends who also came to England that term were given flats to live in around the town. I was the only one from my group placed to live where I would eat my meals and spend time with these people training to be vicars. As a result, Wycliffe is where I met Paul, who became my husband two years later. It was also where I met John Peters, who offered to pray for me and, as a result, the barriers that had built up around me from what had happened received their first mighty blow.

One evening, early on in my time there, I was waiting outside the phone box for it to be free when John walked by. When he asked what I was doing, I explained I had been in a minor car accident before I'd left the US and I had to make a routine call to my insurance company to give them an update on the whiplash in my neck. Immediately John asked if he could pray for my neck. Well, I was a good Christian girl so I said yes, thinking he would add me to his prayer list, like they did back in my Baptist church in St Louis. He had something different in mind though and asked me to find him once I'd finished my call so he could pray for me. I was a little surprised by that – it wasn't how I was used to these things being done – but then I decided to go with it as I was in a different country and I didn't want to be rude.

When I found John later, he asked about my relationship with God and, satisfied by my answer that I was converted, he then asked about my experience of the Holy Spirit. I told him I didn't really have one, though I was familiar with the concept that there was one (I had a lot to learn!)

John then explained that he was going to put his hand on my neck where the whiplash was and ask the Holy Spirit to come and heal it. All I had to do was put my hands out in front of me like I was receiving a gift and be open to God. Again, I didn't want to be rude, and I did believe in prayer, so I did what he asked. Very quickly after he asked the Holy Spirit to come, I started to feel heat in my neck and a weight of peace settled on me. It was then that an image of Beth came to mind, and for the first time since the accident seven years before, I didn't push it down or find a way to distract myself. I let it stay and very gently started to cry. I can't explain why I let it happen then, when I hadn't any other time, other than the presence of God in that moment made me feel safe enough to do it. John asked why I was crying and I told him the story about finding Beth in the bathtub – the first time I'd told anyone. After listening to me, and I'm sure listening to the Holy Spirit at the same time, John told me that even if I'd done it on purpose, I could still be forgiven. "As far as the east is from the west," he said quoting the Psalms,[2] my sins were removed from me. Using the analogy of a piece of broken glass, he said that it was like I'd been clutching that broken glass in the palm of my hand thinking I had to keep hold of it, even though it was causing me damage and pain. The truth was, God wanted me to open my hand to him so he could take that piece of glass from me and heal the damage that had been done by it.

That is exactly what I needed to hear.

Even if I did it on purpose, which of course I didn't, it was just a terrible accident. But even if I did, I could still be forgiven. I, of course, knew this in theory about other people, but it was such a revelation to me personally that it changed everything.

In his love, the Holy Spirit ambushed me, as I like to think of it, and began to set me free. In the following chapters, I'm going to talk more about some of the damaging wounds I'd sustained and how God met me there, bringing his healing and restoration, making it possible for me to join in with him in a life of adventure.

Endnotes

1. *Grace Enough for Three*, Don Clifford (Xulon Press, 2008)
2. Psalm 103:12

Chapter 6
Freedom From Guilt

~

*"As far as the east is from the west, he removes our
transgressions from us."*
(Psalm 103:12)

The Lord touched me through the prayers of someone I'd
just met, and the truth that I could be forgiven even if I'd let
my sister die on purpose was like a wrecking ball making
its first contact with a long established, very strong wall. I'd
lived with so much guilt, and felt it was what I deserved,
that I forgot the promise of forgiveness available to all who
ask. It's the wonderful underlying foundation of truth of
how we can all be free of guilt, no matter what we've done or
how much shame we feel. As 1 John 3:8 says, *"If we confess
and repent, God is faithful to forgive us and purify us from all
unrighteousness."* Or as *The Message* puts it, *"If we admit our
sins – make a clean breast of them – he'll be true to himself.*

He'll forgive our sins and purge us of all wrongdoing." This is the ultimate truth that those of us who struggle with guilt need to embrace.

Having this revelation from God through John was the beginning of freedom – that first crack in my high barrier – but there was still a long way to go to get healing from the damage done through years of carrying the burden of guilt. In order to know how to have freedom from something, it helps to know and understand what it is you're getting freedom from. Let's be clear that we are all guilty when it comes to God's standard. It's worth remembering that Peter's experience of Jesus' supernatural power, when he brought in that miraculous catch of fish in Luke 5, left him acutely aware of his own sinfulness. No one is able to live perfectly, so we all have the effects of sin to deal with in our lives, but we know that Jesus has made provision for us to be rid of the guilt of our sins through the cross. As Christians, we have the great gift of confession, repentance and guaranteed forgiveness. The problem is that, for a variety of reasons, some of us aren't able to move into that place of feeling free from guilt, even if we know in our heads that we are forgiven.

The type of guilt I'm talking about, lived with for so many years, is the feeling of responsibility or remorse for some offence, crime, wrong, etc., whether real or imagined. Along with our own weaknesses in this area, the devil loves to keep us trapped in a place of feeling guilty, because when we are stuck there, we won't be able to grow and develop in the things of God as we should. If we feel guilty, we will almost certainly also feel ashamed and shame makes us hide from others, ourselves, and even God, like Adam and Eve did in the Garden.

My healing has been a gradual process of cooperating with God as he prompts me to look at the next layer of guilt or shame that he wants to deal with, and it's almost always involved having someone pray with me or for me. I think this is partly because involving someone else means I have to talk about it, which was very hard for me in the beginning. Firstly, talking about it brought up the painful and panicky emotions I didn't want to have to feel or experience again. Secondly, I didn't want to make a big deal out of it anyway. I wasn't sure that I, or the situation, was truly important enough to bother someone else with. But that false belief in itself is an effect of guilt and shame. I had to overcome that, and talking and praying through it all with someone else was crucial if I wanted to move on – but that would only come much later.

Living as a prisoner of guilt has many effects – some spiritual, some emotional, some mental and some physical. They won't be exactly the same for everyone, but there will be similarities. One of the tell-tale signs that you struggle with guilt is if you feel like you're going to be found out whenever you see a security guard or member of the police, as if you've done something wrong, when you haven't. This may sound like a trivial thing, but it is symptomatic and it leads to physical manifestations as well, because anytime those feelings surface, anxiety rides on them.

Anxiety sets your body on edge and it reacts in ways that are not healthy: acid in your stomach, tension in your muscles leading to neck, back and, especially in my case, headaches. Meditating on Psalm 37 has really helped me to take control of anxiety as it says repeatedly, *"Do not fret..."* (verses 1, 7, 8). "Fretting", to me, means anxiety. It really spells it out in verse 8 when it says, *"Do not fret, it only leads to evil."* Evil is not just the big obvious acts of darkness, but it's also the smaller, insidious ones, like being physically unwell due to stress. If you're in a complete place of trust and security in God, you won't be experiencing anxiety, worry and stress and your body will be at peace with itself.

Another of the giveaways that someone struggles with guilt is that they are constantly apologising. People with guilt issues will continually be saying sorry, even when they haven't done anything wrong. When you are a prisoner of guilt, you feel at some deep level that everything is somehow your fault.

I can take a situation where something has gone wrong, that is only remotely related to me, and somehow work out how, if I had done things differently, all would have been well. This can even be on a worldwide level – feeling responsible for the problems people live with, things like war, famine, poverty. God has had to teach me that he does not hold me personally accountable for all the world's troubles, and really it's rather arrogant of me to think I have that much influence! He will only hold me accountable for the things he has asked me to do, which, of course, does include working towards a better, fairer world, but he does not expect me to fix everything.

Another aspect of being controlled by guilt is "Survivor's guilt". The term was first used to explain what survivors of the World War II concentration camps were experiencing once they were released. Traumatised and unable to thrive, they couldn't help but feel bad that they had survived when so many others hadn't. Without wishing to trivialise what those people went through in any way, I can identify with survivor's guilt in my own life. I usually end up feeling guilty whenever something is going well for me, but someone else is struggling in the same area. Instead of being grateful for what I have and making the most of it, I feel ashamed of my good fortune and want to downplay it.

The flip-side of feeling responsible for things that go wrong and always apologising, is the tendency to blame others. Now, people can fall into the trap of blaming others for many reasons, but where those who struggle with guilt are concerned, it can happen because always feeling bad about things is so unpleasant that, instead of experiencing those emotions, it's easier to blame somebody else. This can mean that those of us who struggle with guilt can avoid taking personal responsibility when we should. Instead of owning up and saying, "Yeah, I got it wrong," we come up with excuses for why it wasn't our fault. However, if we were in a healthier place in regard to guilt, we wouldn't be threatened by admitting we made a mistake. We would be more able to shrug it off and move on, because it wouldn't take us back into that place of guilt and shame we don't want to visit.

My guilt had a big, destructive effect on me, which manifest itself in me not wanting to take on responsibility for fear of things going wrong. For many years, God had been calling me out to take more of an up-front role with Paul in leading our church, but I turned a deaf ear. I tried all sorts of ways to be obedient to this call, without *actually* being obedient. Finally, I was able to admit to myself that the reason I wouldn't step up and out was because I feared that if I took on responsibility, and was seen to take it on (as I had been doing a lot of it behind the scenes already), I would have to deal with the repercussions when things went wrong. For me, at a deeper level than I was conscious of, I believed that if I was left responsible for something, a tragedy would occur; a tragedy like my sister dying.

This wasn't a rational belief, and if you suggested it to me, I would have said you were being ridiculous and melodramatic. But I now realise it was a controlling belief that held me back and stifled what God was trying to do in me and through me. As long as it was calling the shots, there was no way I could respond to Jesus' invitation to "Come".

Thankfully, God doesn't give up on bringing us healing and wholeness from the damage we experience in life. He is patient and continues to pursue us, even when we get stuck and stubbornly don't want to move on because it's costly to us in terms of emotional pain. Moving through the pain, though, is the way to become free of it. God knows that and patiently leads us through.

The effects of guilt, such as I've described, are clearly damaging emotionally, but they are also very damaging spiritually. As I battled with them, I had little energy or capacity to take on other battles. The foundations of my life were not secure enough to allow me to consider anything that looked like an adventure with God. It took all I had just to keep going. Unresolved emotional issues eat away at our faith. *Can I really trust God? Can I take risks, or will it all go wrong again?*

The ways that I have found freedom from guilt have revolved around staying close to God, spending time in his Word and in worship, and taking little steps of faith, following where I feel he is leading.

You also have to change your thinking and a powerful way of changing wrong thought patterns and ways of behaving is remembering and rehearsing truth – the truth about God and the truth about yourself, in God. There are many scriptures that are good for this and there are lots of resources out there that can help you find ones that fit you and your situation. It's not enough to speak these truths once or twice. You have to take them like medicine, saying them repeatedly, filling yourself up with the truth of God's love for you.

Following on from that, another way to find freedom is to know that you have permission to make mistakes. This is so important because we won't grow and develop beyond a certain point if we are so frightened of failure that we never take any risks. This can be hard, but it is necessary in moving out of the prison of guilt. It is very liberating to know that God would rather have me try and miss the mark than not try at all. If people are disappointed in me or don't approve, it's not the end of the world – I will be stronger and wiser.

———

God has spoken to me about moving out from a place of punishing myself, imprisoned by guilt, through two pictures:

In a time of ministry a few years ago, I had a picture. In it, God was giving me a crown to wear. In the past I would have rejected that straight away, due to feelings of unworthiness, but I'd come far enough by then to accept it. However, I said something along these lines to him:

"Of course, God, I know that as your children there's a crown for all of us. Thank you for mine and, obviously, though it looks perfect on the surface, I know that inside it will be lined with a crown of thorns."

I said that because I truly believed and expected there to be thorns in my crown. It seemed only right and proper that there should be. But, I felt the Lord rebuke me and tell me my crown was definitely not lined with thorns – not now, not ever. Jesus wore a crown of thorns for me and because of his sacrifice, my crown was lined with satin and velvet.

Another time, I felt God lay a churchwarden's staff with a big pearl on the top across my hands. This was interesting as our Anglican church has those sticks in a bracket on the back wall, but they are only ever used for special services when the bishop comes. They are purely ceremonial and symbolic. I knew though, that at one time they represented the churchwardens' authority and it was their role to enforce order in services. They could use those sticks against people and any animals that were being disruptive. In my picture, as God laid the stick across my open hands, it was broken in half. Layers of meaning were in this picture, but one of the significant ones for me was the breaking of a symbol of spiritual punishment. The Lord was saying I was no longer to beat myself spiritually and emotionally because I felt guilty.

Both pictures were about God challenging a wrong image that I had of myself. Guilt leaves us feeling that we are unworthy to carry his authority, and thereby undermines and denies our identity as sons and daughters of the King.

This was, and is still, not easy for me to believe as I know the call to the Christian life is a call to self-sacrifice. I know that as Christians we are called to know the *fellowship of sharing in Christ's sufferings*" (Philippians 3:10), but there is a big difference between self-sacrifice and punishing ourselves for mistakes made in our past. That is living with guilt and it is definitely not part of our calling as Christians. Jesus died to free us from all guilt and condemnation, and that includes the effects of guilt over our mistakes as well.

If there's any guilt you're carrying, bring it to the Lord now. Remember the guarantee given to us in 1 John 3:8, *"If we confess and repent, God is faithful to forgive us and purify us from all unrighteousness."* Take him at his word and know that Jesus died for you. Thank him and tell him (and yourself) that you receive his forgiveness. The next time the guilt starts to resurface, remind yourself that is already dealt with. You've been forgiven and your past cannot define you.

If it's the case though that your guilt has become so familiar to you that you aren't even aware it's there anymore – or, like me, you're trying to go through life detached from it, refusing to acknowledge it's a part of you – then ask the Holy Spirit to highlight it as the burden that it is. Whether you recognise it or not, it will be dragging you down like an overloaded rucksack on your back, filled with unnecessary weight. It will prevent you from stepping out into all God has for you and life will become a hard slog. Once you've been able to do that, then go through the steps listed in the previous paragraph.

You may have to battle with the feelings of guilt for a while, but as you keep telling yourself the truth, they will eventually fade, like that heavy rucksack gradually getting lighter as the unnecessary weight is taken out of it. One day, you will find that you're free and able to run with God.

Chapter 7
Stuck in Suffering

_____

"...to bestow on them a crown of beauty instead of ashes,
the oil of joy instead of mourning and a garment of praise
instead of a spirit of despair."
(Isaiah 61:3)

I know, what a great title for a chapter, "Stuck in Suffering"! Surely no one would choose to get stuck in suffering? Stuck in indecision, stuck in confusion, stuck in apathy are all things I can understand, but stuck in suffering? Wouldn't we do everything in our power to avoid getting stuck in something as obviously unpleasant as suffering?

But, of course, as with all things to do with our inner emotional and spiritual life, it's more complicated than that. Most of us don't consciously choose to suffer, but through our beliefs and choices, that's what can happen.

First of all, let me say that times of suffering are real

and they happen to all of us. *"There is a time to weep and a time to mourn..."* the Bible tells us (Ecclesiastes 3:1). Times of disappointment with life, sickness, trauma, abuse, bereavement are all examples of times of suffering. Some of them can be prolonged, but once the event has passed, we need to do our best to heal and move on. It will often be a gradual moving on – what's important is that it's a moving on in the right direction.

When Moses died at the end of the book of Deuteronomy, the Jewish people mourned him for the prescribed period of time. But then came the moment when God needed them to progress to the next thing, so he said to Joshua, *"Moses my servant is dead. Now then, you and all these people, get ready to cross the Jordan River into the land I am about to give you"* (Joshua 1:2). Without their leader and left to their own devices, the people may have continued to grieve and simply settled where they were, but that wasn't God's best for them, so after a suitable period of time, God gave them a reality check. Yes, Moses is dead, he was saying, but the rest of you aren't and there is more for you to do.

Of course, a time of mourning is necessary and appropriate when someone dies or you've been through a traumatic experience. Grief is real and it is deep and it needs to be fully experienced and expressed in order for us to move on in a healthy way. With some bereavements, we will never fully stop grieving, as that person can never be replaced. But as Christians, we have the hope of seeing our loved ones in the life to come, and the knowledge that God is with us so we can gradually move on from the profound place of grief to the place of acceptance and begin looking forward, as God wanted the Israelites to do.

Sometimes, I find it helpful to think of times of suffering like this: when we go through something difficult in life, whatever it is, we are wounded – the same way a soldier is on the battlefield. Some wounds that soldiers pick up are more serious than others, and some take longer to heal than others. But those that aren't mortal, that don't kill outright, should be treated so that no infection takes hold and so that he or she is given the best chance to fully recover.

That's like the wounds we receive. We are in a spiritual battle, and when we are wounded emotionally, mentally or spiritually (often all three happen at once) we need to guard that we don't pick up an infection that can spread from the wound to the healthy places. An infection like unforgiveness, bitterness, a sense of rejection, shame or self-pity. And even if we are careful not to allow infection to spread, we also need to do what is necessary to allow healing to take place by not denying we are wounded on the one hand, or on the other, by not continually inspecting the wound and, worst of all, metaphorically picking the scabs off it when the wound starts to heal by continually focusing on it.

———

Psalm 84 is another helpful way to look at this subject. It

talks about those whose hearts are set on pilgrimage, and that is all of us who are headed to our ultimate destiny with the Lord in heaven. We are on a journey through this life and our destination is eternity with him.

The psalm says, *"Blessed are those whose strength is in you, who have set their hearts on pilgrimage. As they pass through the Valley of Baca, they make it a place of springs; the Autumn rains also cover it with pools. They go from strength to strength, till each appears before God in Zion"* (verses 5-7).

The Valley of Baca, mentioned here, is commonly agreed by Hebrew scholars to mean the Valley of Weeping, so I'd like to insert that word this time:

"Blessed are those whose strength is in you, who have set their hearts on pilgrimage. As they pass through the Valley of Weeping, they make it a place of springs; the Autumn rains also cover it with pools. They go from strength to strength, till each appears before God in Zion."

The Valley of Weeping sounds a lot like a time of suffering to me and, according to this psalm, it's a place through which we all must pass on our way to appearing before God in Zion. The question we have to ask ourselves is, have we, in any way, set up camp and decided to settle in the Valley of Weeping instead of passing through it?

And if we have... *why?*

A big reason we might settle is that we can't see our way out of the Valley. It stretches as far as the eye can see and we lose hope that there's something better ahead. So we decide to stop where we are, hunker down and not bother carrying on.

This must have been a temptation for David in the years between being a shepherd and being crowned king. In those years he was exiled, hunted and betrayed. Among many other difficult things, he had to hide out in caves and was forced to feign insanity in order to stay alive. This was a time of real hardship for David and he could have given up on God and become embittered. Instead, we see throughout the Psalms that, although he would have a good old moan from time to time, he continued to keep the faith and was determined to keep going with God.

In Psalm 71 there's a great example of this. He says,
"Deliver me, my God, from the hand of the wicked, from the grasp of those who are evil and cruel.

For you have been my hope, Sovereign Lord, my confidence since my youth. From my birth I have relied on you; you brought me forth from my mother's womb. I will ever praise you.

I have become a sign to many; you are my strong refuge. My mouth is filled with your praise, declaring your splendour all day long.

Do not cast me away when I am old; do not forsake me when my strength is gone. For my enemies speak against me; those who wait to kill me conspire together. They say, 'God has forsaken him; pursue him and seize him, for no one will rescue him.'

Do not be far from me, my God; come quickly, God, to help me. May my accusers perish in shame; may those who want to harm me be covered with scorn and disgrace." (verses 4-13)

David is obviously going through a hard time and is free to tell God all about it. However, he continues with this great statement: *"As for me, I shall always have hope; I will praise you more and more"* (verse 14). "As for me, I shall always have hope" – that's an incredible declaration – and because he held on to hope, David has become a sign to all succeeding generations of what a life of worship and intimacy with God can look like. He understood that God does not mean for us to do more than pass through the Valley of Weeping on our way to somewhere better.

Once, when I was praying for a friend who had past battles with depression and was currently going through a really hard time, I felt the Lord show me that she had a choice in her present circumstances. The fact was, she felt like she was in a cave, having to feel her way forward in the pitch dark, not sure where she was heading or if she would ever get out. Her choice was to either give up and huddle down in the dark, not risking staying engaged with life, or to be brave and keep feeling her way forward. I knew God was saying that if she didn't give up, but held on to hope and participated with all that was going on around her, rather than withdrawing and shutting down, her time in the cave would soon be over. She was near the exit, but had to keep going to find it.

Fortunately, she made the choice to keep trusting God and to stay open to others. Before long, her circumstances changed dramatically for the better.

We must to keep our hearts open to hope – that will keep us from getting stuck in suffering.

Another reason we may set up camp in the Valley of Weeping is because it can feel disloyal to move on, especially if we are suffering due to either bereavement or we're struggling with survivor's guilt.

If you have lost someone close to you, moving on from your grief and moving on with your life can feel like a betrayal of all they meant to you, but that isn't true. As I mentioned at the beginning of the chapter, when Moses died, the nation mourned, but then the time came when God said they were ready for the next step on their journey, and it's the same with us.

Grief is like the ocean at high tide – it comes in waves, sometimes threatening to drown us. It takes all our concentration and energy to cope with surviving it, but eventually the waves recede as the tide goes out and we're more able to withstand it, and we have the energy to begin to think about other things. That's when we need to listen to God's voice and be willing to step out as he guides us.

If you struggle with survivor's guilt, then you can feel you owe it to those who didn't make it or weren't as fortunate as you to stay put and suffer. If that's you, you need to understand the difference between true guilt and false guilt, as described in the last chapter. True guilt is dealt with at the cross. It's something we confess, and then we receive our forgiveness and move on. False guilt is a feeling of condemnation that traps us in a spiral of shame. It is a lie we believe about ourselves that we must fight to break free from or it will keep us imprisoned. That has been true for me.

I have been hugely helped in my journey of healing in this, and other areas, by being involved in something called the Healing Prayer School, a week-long course of teaching and prayer ministry run by Lin Button, and hosted once a year at our church.[1] I started out as a participant on the school and since then have been a part of the team.

Originally, I went along as a participant because I knew I really needed help to move on. Although my barriers had been breached, they were still intact enough to stop me from stepping out and I didn't know what else to do to help myself, so I signed up and went along to the course.

Many things impacted me that week, but one thing Lin said took my breath away. It was a simple sentence, but the implication of it was life changing for me. Her exact words were, "Some of you need to know that you have the right to exist." Immediately I knew I was one of those, because in my heart of hearts, I didn't really believe it.

Lin explained that in a family where there has been a death of one of the children, the surviving siblings may struggle with feeling it's OK to live and thrive. This made a lot of sense to me and helped me understand my situation – from my parents having lost a child and having a still birth before I came along, to then having a little sister who needed 24 hour care in my preschool years who then died, and then Beth demanding a lot of time and attention and then her death.

My family's history made it hard for any of us to process the feelings that we carried. Particularly for me, the inability to believe I had the right to exist was worse because of feeling responsible for Beth's accident and death. Since that first Healing Prayer School, I have practised telling myself I do have the right to exist, and I can say I've mostly come to the point of really believing it. I see it like blowing up a deflated balloon. At first it's hard to tell if all the effort you're expending is making any difference, but if you carry on, you'll begin to notice a change and the balloon will gradually inflate until it is more solid and substantial, just like the process that went on inside of me.

As discussed in the last chapter, living with persistent guilt is another way of being stuck in suffering. About 10 years after my sister Beth died, Paul and I decided to marry. Moving to England permamently was an easy decision in some ways, but in others, a very hard one. Some of the hard parts are what you would expect – leaving family, friends and culture behind – but what was really hard was the immense guilt I felt. My mother didn't want me to leave and even said to me at one point that God had already taken three children from her, how could he take another?

Her saying that wasn't enough to stop me from carrying on with my relationship with Paul, but it was more than enough to make me feel horrendously bad about it. I already believed I was responsible for one of her children dying and here I was making it worse by leaving myself. The week after we were married, I cried pretty much the whole plane journey from the US to England, and not a tear of that was because I felt sad for myself (those tears came later with homesickness). I was crying because I felt so bad about what I was putting my mother through.

The feeling of guilt was one I was so accustomed to that I wasn't even that aware of it, and I certainly wasn't aware of how it controlled me. However, here I am 25 years after leaving the US, finally having moved on and knowing a degree of freedom from controlling guilt and with a definite determination to keep pursuing greater freedom from it.

I was able to break free from the guilt and the shame I felt through lots of prayer, support from others, God's revelation and my determination. And I say determination because it can be hard to move on. Facing and feeling the pain of what you've been carrying, so God can heal and redeem it, is hard and you have to have courage to move on from the familiar, albeit uncomfortable place, to a new unknown place.

We can also get stuck in suffering because it's either too painful or too scary to keep moving. It can be too painful because, as I said earlier, we have to allow ourselves to feel what we've kept hidden and buried, and we may have to let go of things that have been important or represented security to us. It can be too scary, especially if we've experienced some kind of trauma in our past, as we may be fearful of anything that is unknown and, let's face it, the future is always unknown. You can end up with what Joyce Meyer calls "evil forebodings" where you think every message and every phone call is going to deliver bad news. You're constantly on the alert for something going wrong and expect a catastrophe around every corner.

I have struggled with evil forebodings, where I always expected the worst to happen – partly to do with my personality, but a lot more to do with my past. I've had to learn to let God minister healing to me, and I have to do my part by taking those thoughts captives when they come, as the Apostle Paul tells us (2 Corinthians 10:5), replacing them with positive truths about God and my identity in him.

The Apostle Paul has a lot to tell us about our thought life and if we simply put what he says into practice, we'd go a long way to getting unstuck from suffering. As well as telling us in 2 Corinthians 10:5 to *"take wrong thoughts captive and make them obedient to Christ"*, or as *The Message* translation puts it, *"We use our powerful God-tools for smashing warped philosophies, tearing down barriers erected against the truth of God, fitting every loose thought and emotion and impulse into the structure of life shaped by Christ"*, Paul also tells us in Romans 12 to *"not conform to the pattern of the world, but to be transformed by the renewing of our minds. Then we will be able to test and approve what God's will is – his good, pleasing and perfect will"* (Romans 12:2).

Again, *The Message* translation is helpful in presenting these familiar verses in a fresh way:

"Don't become so well adjusted to your culture that you fit into it without even thinking. Instead, fix your attention on God. You'll be changed from the inside out. Readily recognise what he wants from you, and quickly respond to it. Unlike the culture around you, always dragging you down to its level of immaturity. God brings out the best in you, develops well-formed maturity in you."

So, we need to recognise when we're slipping into wrong thinking, stop it and confront it with truth about God. We may even need to change harmful patterns of thinking that are keeping us stuck and stagnant. We can do this by calling to mind the goodness of God and his love for us. That is what David continually did in his psalms and it can change our whole outlook and allow God to move in our lives.

For Christmas I was given a beautifully written and profound book called *One Thousand Gifts*[2]. Ann Voskamp, the author, tells of how she sought to begin living a life of "eucharisteo", which basically means living a life of thankfulness (the Greek word *eucharisteo* literally means "thanksgiving" and has within it the Greek words for "grace" and "joy".)

From Ann's writing, it is obvious that she was stuck in a place of suffering, struggling at points in her life with depression and self-harm. But when she was challenged to make a list of one thousand things she was thankful for, her life dramatically changed. Not overnight, but gradually as she learned to recognise and then more fully trust in God's love and goodness.

When thinking about the implications of what Jesus says in John 6:29, which says, in the Amplified translation, *"This is the work (service) that God asks of you: that you believe in the One Whom He has sent (that you cleave to, trust, rely on, and have faith in His Messenger)"*, she says:

"That's my daily work, the work God asks of me? To trust. The work I shirk. To trust in the Son, to trust in the wisdom of this moment, to trust in now. And trust is that: *work*. The work of trusting love. Intentional and focused. Sometimes, too often, I don't want to muster the energy. Stress and anxiety seem easier. Easier to let a mind run wild with the worry than to exercise discipline..." (p147).

And there we are back to taking our thoughts captive. Don't let them run wild. Use self-control and discipline to rein them in and redirect them.

Later on in the book, she describes the difference between lament – a cry of belief in a good God – and complaint – the bitter howl of unbelief in any benevolent God in this moment. She says that after a bad day she may feel disappointment and even despair, "but to give thanks is an action and rejoice is a verb and these are not mere pulsing emotions. While I may not always feel joy, God asks me to give thanks in all things, because He knows that the feeling of joy begins in the action of thanksgiving."

"True saints," she says, "know that the place where all joy comes from is far deeper than that of feelings; joy comes from the place of the very presence of God. Joy is God and God is joy and joy doesn't negate all other emotions – joy transcends all other emotions" (p176).

Living a life of thankfulness moved Ann on from the Valley of Weeping so she could continue her pilgrimage, going from strength to strength, and it will do the same for us.[3]

It's sometimes said that the opposite of faith is unbelief, but a more accurate observation would be that the opposite of faith is fear. Faith is the confident, joyful expectation of good things. Fear, by contrast, is the anxious anticipation of bad things happening. When we learn to praise God for what he is doing – and he's always at work in a way that blesses us – then it is so much easier for our faith to rise. Praise and thanksgiving release us from the pain of the past, moves us on from suffering, and prepare us for the blessings that lie ahead.

Endnotes
1. www.healingprayerschool.org.uk

2. *One Thousand Gifts*, Ann Voskamp (Zondervan, 2011)

3. Another author I've found incredibly helpful is Brené Brown, who has done groundbreaking research on shame and vulnerability. I have read all four of her books and found each one enormously helpful. I highly recommend them to anyone who wants to know greater freedom from guilt and shame, or is simply looking for more joy and freedom in their life.

Chapter 8
The Betrayal Barrier

"Consider it pure joy, my brothers and sisters, whenever you face trials of many kinds..."
(James 1:2)

"All Christians experience disappointment but 90% never get over the betrayal barrier."[1] That's a quote from R.T. Kendall and in my experience, it's true. The disappointment that comes when we feel betrayed by God is one of the biggest and most common barriers to stepping out to join Jesus. We find it hard to move on when we believe God has let us down. Or, if we won't allow ourselves to think that way about God, we find it hard to move on when life hasn't lived up to our expectations. If we're Christians though, and believe God is in control of our lives, we will most likely hold him responsible for where we feel our life has gone wrong, whether we acknowledge it or not, and that's where the betrayal barrier comes in. It's a large part of why so many Christians don't live the life of Kingdom adventure God always intended for us, and why we don't have the impact on the world around us that we should.

Joyce Meyer says, "When things don't prosper or succeed according to our plan, the first emotion we feel is disappointment. This is normal. There is nothing wrong with feeling disappointed. But we must know what to do with that feeling, or it will move into something more serious."[2]

This was brought home to me just the other day when I was walking home. Wherever you look in Woodford, there are horse chestnut trees. They line the High Road and the pedestrian paths – they are everywhere and they are beautiful, majestic trees. I can understand why someone decided to plant rows of them. In the Spring they are a vibrant green, with striking flowers that look like candles, and in the Autumn, they drop their smooth, round nut that children love to collect and play "conkers" with.

The sad thing is that in the last five years or so, all these trees have become diseased. Most of the year, they look fine and do what they're supposed to do, but about mid-June, the disease starts to show itself. Brown spots appear on the leaves and in another month, they will be mostly shriveled and dead, looking terrible. It won't be until the other trees start to lose all their leaves a couple of months later that the horse chestnuts will once again blend in. There's something wrong on the inside of them. Though they look good most of the time, the disease will show itself in due course, causing premature death to the leaves and, as a result, affecting the lifecycle of the tree. Eventually, if the disease isn't dealt with, the trees will simply die because they aren't able to take in all the nourishment they need through their leaves.

That's a lot like us. We can look good for a season, but if there's something diseased in us, like guilt or disappointment that has grown into something more rooted and serious, it will start to show and we won't flourish as God intends us to.

There are many ways for disappointment to enter our lives: it can come through relationship breakdown, abuse, illness (whether our own or that of someone we care about); it can come through sudden tragedy, through loss of employment, bereavement, or unmet expectations. These are things that are common to all of us. In fact, Jesus promised us that, *"In this world you will have trouble..."* (John 16:33).

These struggles are a part of life and if we don't move on from them, we will get stuck in that place of disappointment, which will lead to discouragement, which will lead to depression, which will lead to despair. The good news is that Jesus didn't stop at promising us we'd have trouble – he carried on to instruct us to, "Take heart" or to "Cheer up" as he has overcome the world. God is always wanting to meet us in our place of disappointment and *re-appoint* us. He's always willing to comfort us and give us fresh vision and hope, but we have to be willing to face the pain and make the journey with him.

That's been my experience as God has met me in my place of deep disappointment over my sister's death. I've also had struggles since then in other areas, but I know that those challenges were made worse because of my hesitance in dealing with the earlier wound in my life. For example, moving to England from America was a big adjustment for me, which wasn't helped by Paul being ordained at the same time into the Church of England, which was more foreign to me in some ways, coming from a Baptist background, than the UK was to me as an American.

I knew God had called me to England and to marry Paul. We'd both spent a lot of time seeking the Lord over our future together during our almost two year long-distance relationship. I was constantly bothering God, asking him to help me make the right decision, listing all the pros and cons, telling him my hopes and fears. One day when I was mid-litany yet again, God broke in unmistakably and said to me, "I will use you and Paul together for my kingdom."

I can tell you this shut me up and made me think. It reminded me that God has a bigger agenda than my personal hopes and fears – his kingdom. I took him at his word for a day or two, but then I was right back to my repeated prayers and carried on with them until our wedding day – it's a good thing God is so patient with us. (I never told anyone what God said to me until I told Paul when we made the decision to marry). So, I knew from the beginning that God was in, and for, our relationship, but I found it so lonely and difficult to start with.

Paul was ordained eight weeks after we were married and we moved to Moreton on the Wirral for his curacy. I went through such a degree of culture shock that I decided I must have heard God wrong. That then led me to question if God was there at all, because if he was, he didn't seem to care too much that I was missing my family, friends and everything else I was familiar with. I never regretted marrying Paul, but the adjustment to life in a new country was hard.

For one thing, it was so cold (I grew up in the Midwest of America, over 1000 miles from the ocean, with temperatures in the summer of 30 degrees and above being the norm. Now I was a mile from the Irish Sea with its cold breeze constantly blowing). Also, the person I knew the longest there was Paul, and to be honest, we'd spent most of our time on different continents. So I had no history there with anyone and I quickly lost my sense of identity (which wasn't that strong to start with).

It was during this period that I learned the importance of having an attitude of gratitude and benefitted from studying the life of Joseph. Sold into slavery by his brothers, falsely accused, spending years in prison even though he was innocent, being forgotten about by someone he'd helped, Joseph had been through it all. Yet, throughout his journey he kept a good attitude and didn't blame God. At the end of his story, he tells his brothers that although they meant to harm him, he knew God had meant it for good.[3] He never seemed to hit the betrayal barrier as far as God was concerned and I found that inspiring and challenging. Helped by this, gradually I adjusted to life in England. I've even made my peace with the Church of England.

That leads me to another challenge, which has been learning to cope with the limitations that having children with additional needs places on our family.

Both our children are on the autistic spectrum. Rachel is very high-functioning and able to hold her own through most of life, but Joshua has severe special needs. He's now officially an adult, having recently turned 18, but apart from his size and chronological age, most everything else about him is on a toddler level.

Having a child with these needs has been a challenge and another chance to overcome the betrayal barrier in several different ways. First there was the need to let go of all the unmet expectations. I thought I didn't have too many expectations when Joshua was born. I decided that I wouldn't place expectations on my children to go to university or get married. What I didn't realise was that I had a whole list of unspoken expectations. After all, I did expect them to be able to talk, to learn to read and write, make friends, tell us their hopes and dreams, etc.

When that didn't happen (and it still hasn't 18 years later) we had to grieve and let go of what we wouldn't have with Joshua and accept and learn to celebrate what we did have.

This hasn't always been easy, but God is faithful and he has provided help and support and he has helped us to grow stronger through it.

Studying Job a few years ago really taught me several important lessons. In a nutshell, Job loses everything through no fault of his own, but in the end God restores him and he ends up with double of all that he lost.

What impressed me about Job was that with all he went through, he never blamed God. He did question and complain, but he never blamed. At his very lowest, he still said, *"Blessed be the name of the Lord"* (Job 1:21 ESV). This was a challenge to me, but by disciplining myself to praise God and to say that he is good when things are hard, I have developed much stronger spiritual muscles. God is more able to help me in the battles I face, because I am trusting him through them rather than blaming him for them.

I had a dream once that helped me understand this. It was the night before Easter and Joshua wasn't sleeping at all. In fact, he was making so much noise that no one else was sleeping either. I kept asking God to make him go to sleep. Easter is a big day in church, after all, and I knew Paul would have a full day of preaching in three services, along with all the other duties that go with being a vicar. I told God all the reasons it would be unhelpful for us to be tired the next day. Nothing changed though and after a couple of hours, I decided I would try a new tack and started to sing the song, "Blessed Be the Name of the Lord" over and over in my head. It wasn't long after I made that decision – I was on my third or fourth time through – that Joshua went quiet. I went to sleep and began dreaming.

In my dream, Paul and I were side by side in one of those boats that have pedals for your feet. We were both pedalling and the boat was moving through the water. I was aware though, that in the water itself were pirates who were looking for the chance to get us and hurt us. I knew with the kind of certainty you have in dreams, that as long as we were in the boat, we were completely safe, but if we ended up in the water, we were fair game for the pirates.

I shouted out, "Paul, we're shipping water," as I became aware we had somehow sprung a leak and the boat was filling up, threatening to sink and giving us to the pirates if we didn't do something quick. We began bailing the water out, using all our strength to stay afloat. Before long I heard the sound of a bugle in the distance and I knew that the cavalry were coming to our rescue. I was filled with relief as I knew we were now safe and then I woke up.

I believe that dream represented what had taken place spiritually when I chose to worship rather than to keep asking God over and over to make Joshua go to sleep, getting more and more disappointed when nothing seemed to change. That disappointment, which so easily becomes self-pity, was the leak allowing us to take on water, bringing us closer and closer to the pirates' territory. When we began to bail out the boat, that was like my decision to praise God, even though it was hard work, and it allowed God to come to our rescue.

I learned a powerful lesson from that experience and now know that worship is the most powerful tool we have once we ask God for what we need. In our disappointment, the enemy uses our circumstances to say that God doesn't know about us or care about us. Worship expresses faith. It says that God is good and it makes space for him to move in our circumstances. I recommend it as a great resource and antidote to disappointment and self-pity.

• ～～

I have to say that dealing with your disappointment or overcoming the betrayal barrier doesn't have to be done publicly in a ministry time, but if in that sort of setting, you find you're wanting to escape because you don't like the feelings that surface, you need to make a decision to seek out help and prayer support. God is not being mean by asking us to deal with our stuff – he's showing great kindness by pursuing us to bring us the wholeness he always meant for us to have. He bought it for us by sending Jesus to die on the cross, which means he can be with us through his Spirit, our comfort, counsellor, guide and teacher.

Often, it will take time and determination to come to a place of healing, but the end result is worth it, both for ourselves and God's kingdom. Disappointment will prevent you from stepping out of the boat. You'll have a reduced expectation of good things happening, and live with the refusal to risk, because of a heightened expectation of bad things. Disappointment may not sound that serious, but how much is it making us miss out on?

Endnotes

1. R.T. Kendall has written several great books on the subject of forgiveness, including *Total Forgiveness* (Hodder and Stoughton, 2003).
2. *Straight Talk on Depression: Overcoming Emotional Battles with the Power of God's Word*, Joyce Meyer (FaithWords, 2008).
3. Genesis 50:20.

Chapter 9
Restored by the Spirit

"He restores my soul."
(Psalm 23:3)

What does it mean to be "restored"? When we use the word "restore", it's often in the context of buildings or works of art – things that need to be returned to their original state because the effects of time, and often human intervention, have caused their true character to be lost or hidden.

If you looked at a painting that was in the process of being restored, you might see parts that showed the effects of time – a film of tobacco and accumulated dirt, paint that had faded in the light – but in other parts, where the restorer had been at work, you might see the original, as its creator intended. The artist who painted the picture meant for it to be put on display. He or she took care when they created it and paid attention to detail.

If you've spent much time around the church, that might remind you of a verse from Ephesians which says, *"We are God's handiwork..."* (other versions say "workmanship" or "masterpiece") *"...created in Christ Jesus to do good works, which God prepared in advance for us to do"* (Ephesians 2:10).

We were created by God with care and attention to detail and we are meant to be on display for him. But like that painting, we are affected by the environment we're in and we will pick up what is in the atmosphere around us. So, we all need to be *restored* regularly from those effects. The world, our culture, sin – they take a toll on us and we require constant cleaning.

If I'm not in the regular habit of asking the Holy Spirit to *"search me and know my heart"* (Psalm 139:23), asking him to *"see if there is any offensive way in me and lead me in the way everlasting"*, then I am in danger of accumulating more and more dirt, until what my Creator intended me to be is covered up and hidden; and the good works he prepared for me to do won't get done. However, if I do ask the Holy Spirit to search me and know my heart, and I confess where I've got it wrong and where my attitudes are not what they should be, and I then receive his forgiveness and love for me afresh, I'm preventing that film of dirt and grime from building up in me. Instead, the real me, the "me" God intended, can be more fully displayed.

Sometimes, though, a work of art can't be restored by a

simple cleaning, because the damage done to it is more than the accumulation of dirt and grime. There have been many attempts to restore "The Last Supper" painted by Leonardo da Vinci in the late 15th century, but because of the way it was painted and the materials used, much of it has been lost. Around sixty years after da Vinci had completed the piece, it started to deteriorate. The figures had already begun to lose their distinctiveness. The first attempt at restoration was made in the early 1700s, but this did not go well. Around fifty years later, that restoration work was stripped and a new attempt was made. But, due to public outrage, this attempt was stopped as the restorer had repainted all but three of the disciples' faces. He was basically repainting it, substituting his own figures, as he went along.

You see, only the original creator could restore that work of art to its true character (we might even say its "true glory"). Of course, that's impossible for this piece of art as da Vinci has been dead for over 500 years. His unique ability was lost to the world as soon as he died. The good news is though, when we have damage done to us beyond the usual result of the pollution of our environment, we do have our original Creator, who can restore us to our true character/ glory, which is, after all, a reflection of his.

When Jesus was on earth, he went about reversing the damage done to people. I love that several of his healing miracles use the word "restored" to describe what he did. In Matthew 9:27-28 it says, *"As Jesus went on from there, two blind men followed him, calling out, 'Have mercy on us, Son of David!' When he had gone indoors, the blind men came to him, and he asked them, 'Do you believe I am able to do this?' 'Yes, Lord,' they replied. Then he touched their eyes and said, 'According to your faith will it be done to you,' and their sight was restored."*

In Matthew 12, when the religious leaders were trying to catch Jesus out and find something they could use against him, Jesus decided to make it a teaching moment to demonstrate something of God's nature which they, in their religious mindset, had lost sight of. It was the Sabbath, a day set apart by the 4th Commandment, when Jesus offended them by healing a man. I don't think the man who was healed was feeling very offended, but those who were using religious laws to control people were very offended.

"He (Jesus) went into their synagogue, and a man with a shriveled hand was there. Looking for a reason to accuse Jesus, they asked him, 'Is it lawful to heal on the Sabbath?' He said to them, 'If any of you has a sheep and it falls into a pit on the Sabbath, will you not take hold of it and lift it out? How much more valuable is a man than a sheep! Therefore it is lawful to do good on the Sabbath.' Then he said to the man, 'Stretch out your hand.' So he stretched it out and it was completely restored, just as sound as the other." (Matthew 12:9-13).

Luke 8 doesn't use the word "restored", but I love the picture it paints of the man involved. We first see him when Jesus and his disciples get out of their boat. It says that

Jesus was met by a demon-possessed man from the town. It then goes on to describe how this poor man lived a solitary existence among the tombs, wearing no clothes. He was well-known by the people of the area, as Mark tells us how they had tried to bind him, but no chains could hold him and he would cry out and cut himself with stones.

Along comes Jesus who casts out the demons from him and the next thing you know, this man who was tormented to the point of being completely isolated from society, driven to wandering naked through a cemetery, shouting out and committing daily self-harm, is now seen sitting at Jesus' feet, dressed and in his right mind. That is such a beautiful picture of the restoration Jesus brings.

Jesus, who came as God's son and lived out his earthly ministry fully under the power and direction of the Holy Spirit, was able to reverse the damage that had been done to people, returning them to their original state. And I don't just mean back to the original state of each individual before they lost their sight or lived a life that allowed them to be severely demonised, but back to the state of the original creation, back in the Garden of Eden, when there was unbroken connection between God the Creator and his creation; before sin and then death, shortly after, entered the picture.

Jesus came to show us God's love and what his kingdom looks like – a kingdom of life, healing and freedom from fear. Then he died as a sacrifice, so that all that got in the way of our relationship with God could be removed. Then he came back to life and returned to heaven to send the Holy Spirit to every human being who allows him access to their life.

Back to Ephesians 2:10 – if we are created not just as God's handiwork, but also to join in with God's work, then we must believe that he can and will work through us. Unfortunately, the damage that has been done to his image in us also prevents us from stepping out of the boat and joining him. Rather than being confident in God, most of us battle with insecurity.

As children of God, we more than anyone else ought to live our lives from a place of security and confidence. One of my favourite verses, Isaiah 30:15, highlights two things which our relationship with him provides: *"In repentance and rest is your salvation, in quietness and trust is your strength."* Salvation and strength: knowing you're saved and knowing you're strong – are fundamental to living well. However, many of us are actually living from a place of imprisoning insecurity and uncertainty. That's not God's best for us and it's certainly not his best for the world, because if we as Christians, who know the love and care of God, can't live secure lives, what hope is there for anyone else?

Insecurity kills off faith and feeds fear. Beth Moore has a great book called, *So Long, Insecurity*[1], in which she quotes a very good definition of insecurity from another book called *The Tender Heart* by Joseph Nowinski. It says, "Insecurity refers to a profound sense of self-doubt – a deep feeling of uncertainty about our basic worth and our place in the world ... The insecure man or woman lives in constant fear of rejection and a deep uncertainty about whether his or her own feelings and desires are legitimate."

That fear and uncertainty may manifest itself in a variety of ways: gossip, comparison, busyness, prejudice, negativity, people-pleasing, withdrawing and passivity. It depends on our personality (and our coping and defence mechanisms when insecurity kicks in) which of those we experience at any given time. I've lived a lot of my life with high degrees of insecurity and I can put my hand up to several of those. I've really had to work hard, with God's help, to overcome them. I'm still a work in progress, as we all are, but I'm a lot better than I used to be and I trust God to continue to help and heal me.

The problem is, it's easy to be insecure, to carry around in us that profound sense of self-doubt. Not only does it come naturally to us, we can so easily reinforce insecurity in each other. For sure, culture constantly assaults our sense of security, exploiting any weakness it can find. The beauty industry for instance, which is worth billions each year, is built on making women, and increasingly men, feel bad about themselves. It's nothing new – I found this deodorant advert from the 1920s which is good example of how undermining some advertising can be:

"You're a pretty girl, Mary, and you're smart about most things. But you're just a bit stupid about yourself. You love a good time – but you seldom have one. Evening after evening you sit at home alone. You've met several grand men, who seem interested at first. They took you out once – and that was that. Wake up, Mary..."

Poor Mary, she didn't stand a chance…

4 out of 10 adverts try to sell to you by letting you know that there is something about you that needs improving and now we are directly targeted through our online history. It is hard work to not succumb to the feeling of "not being good enough" when you're continually being told that you aren't good enough. However, the good news is that there is a way that we can grow in the security of knowing that we *are* good enough, not just when it comes to reacting to advertising, but in every other area of life as well.

It is our challenge as Christians to recognise when we are living from an imprisoning place of insecurity. Sadly, that isn't as easy as it sounds. We can be so accustomed to our prisons that we think it's normal to feel, live, and act the way we do in them – to such an extent that we don't even realise we're in a prison. Or, we may have decided that there's no hope that things can ever change, so we do our best to make ourselves comfortable in our imprisonment. But, God is always calling us out of our prisons to a place of freedom. We have to cooperate with him in order to overcome our insecurities and be free to enter into all he has for us.

I am not a sailor, but I do understand the principle of how a sail is used to harness the power of the wind to propel the boat in the right direction. For this process to work, the sails need to be in good condition, with no holes, no tears and no fraying around the edges. That sort of damage stops the sail from being as effective as it should be. For us, our insecurities are like the holes, tears and fraying of a sail, preventing us from catching the full power of the wind of the Spirit. This stops us from being all we can be, because much of what God wants to do in us and through us is lost. Honestly, it takes a lot of discipline and hard work to get, and then to keep, our sails in good condition. They can be damaged even before we're born. From the time of conception we are vulnerable to our sails being torn. Many of our insecurities will be well in place before we even grow past our early years as we deal with what life throws at us. The good news is it's never too late to confront those things and overcome them with God's help.

Your story won't be the same as mine, but you will have had things in your life that have damaged you emotionally, mentally and spiritually.[2] In my experience, too many people would prefer to pretend that they haven't been wounded or damaged in any way. There are many reasons why we choose to behave this way. Cultural expectations of self-sufficiency stop us from feeling we have permission to ask for help, or cause us to believe it's weak to admit we are struggling with feelings of insecurity or inadequacy. Some theologies of "victorious Christian living" are profoundly unhelpful. There's also the denial that the things we experience shape us. You can deny it all you want, but if you're human, the repercussions of what has gone on in your life will ripple out and affect the way you live, including your attitudes towards yourself and others and, most importantly, your relationship with God.

But I think the biggest reason we choose to ignore the things that damage us is that it can be truly unpleasant and really hard work to deal with them in a healthy, healing way. There is no shortcut to emotional healing – we have to let the pain we've buried to surface, so that God can redeem it. He can't heal what we hide and once we have allowed him to touch those things with his love and grace, we then have to walk out that healing, which can be equally challenging.

God is always pursuing us to bring us healing and wholeness. He can repair our sails, he can even give us brand new sails, if that's what he decides to do, and we allow him to.

I once had a dream that a huge wave, like a tsunami, was coming. It was higher than the tallest buildings and was travelling towards me. In my dream, everyone had their own inflatable to keep them afloat when the wave came. Some had beach balls, others had lilos, etc. I ran to find my inflatable and when I got to it, it was a lifeboat, but it had a hole in it so was completely deflated. As I realised this, I woke up.

I recognised all too well the truth of that dream. I had a hole in me that meant I leaked out whatever God filled me with on a regular basis. Praying with a friend about this, I asked God to repair my hole, but I felt him say to me that he could make it so that it was like the hole had never existed. I told him I had my doubts about that, but then I remembered Sarah laughing when she overheard Abraham being told they would have a child in their old age. She was rebuked and asked, *"Is anything too hard for the Lord?"* (Genesis 18:14). So, I decided to agree that yes, he could make it as though the hole had never existed. And I know if he can do it for me, he can do it for you.

Going back to Isaiah 30:15, *"In repentance and rest is your salvation, in quietness and trust is your strength"*... Salvation and strength. This verse assures me that once I say sorry for anything I've done wrong or feel bad about, I then have to rest, settle into and believe in God's mercy and forgiveness; that is my salvation. My strength comes from an inner peace, quietness and trust in God's goodness and love for me that isn't showy or flashy, but is nevertheless the real thing. That is true security and freedom.

Sadly, this passage in Isaiah continues, *"But you would have none of it. You said, 'No, we will flee on horses. Therefore you will flee! You will ride off on swift horses.' Therefore your pursuers will be swift! A thousand will flee at the threat of one; at the threat of five you will flee away, till you are left like a flagstaff on a mountaintop, like a banner on a hill"* (verses 15b-17).

That sounds like serious insecurity. I know that God was talking through Isaiah to Israel about external enemies, but it speaks to us as well. We can easily decide we would rather flee in our insecurity than have God's salvation and strength, making us easy prey for the enemy. We can become timid and afraid in that place of self-doubt and fear of rejection and then run away at the smallest threat. We are left an empty, hollow shell of what we should be, like a lonely flagstaff or banner left representing nothing, or a tattered sail full of holes, unable to catch the wind. With God's help and healing though, we don't have to react that way. We can choose God's salvation and strength and stand firm.

The really great news is that this passage ends with the reassuring promise that, as soon as we turn to him, God welcomes us: *"Yet the Lord longs to be gracious to you; he rises to show you compassion. For the Lord is a God of justice. Blessed are all who wait for him!"* (Isaiah 30:18)

In my experience, God will restore us, but wants us to play our part. Wait for the Lord, let him search you, and then surrender. Deal with anything that the Spirit highlights or challenges you on, accepting his help. Almost always you will have to accept other people's help as well. Read the Bible and learn more about God's character and about your identity as his child. When the lies of insecurity come, the self-doubt and fears of uncertainty and rejection, they must be confronted with the truth. I have to say that I don't know anyone who has overcome a major insecurity in their life who didn't have to repeat the truth to themselves in order to replace the lies they were in the habit of believing. You have to make a new neural pathway in your brain and that can take time and determination, but if you don't give up, your thinking will change. As I said before, it's like taking medicine – it doesn't always taste nice and you often can't tell that it's making any difference, but if you complete the course, there will be an end result.

———

The Holy Spirit is God's Spirit everywhere, all the time, the Third Person of the Trinity, looking for opportunities to restore his creation back to his original design. He can do it in an instant, like those healings in the gospels, but sometimes it takes time because he's waiting for us to do our part in cooperating with our restoration. Sometimes he takes his time because he's being kind to us, understanding us better than we understand ourselves. He knows that we may need time to adjust, like when a bright light is turned on after we've been in the dark. It can be painful and we have to wait for our eyes to adjust to the light.

I've experienced the Spirit's work in my life in all those ways. In fact, it was only a couple of years ago at New Wine that I felt God really spoke to me about the work of restoration he had been doing in my life over many years. I was prayed for in a celebration and had a powerful encounter with the Lord. At first I didn't know what he was doing, but I've learned to allow the Spirit to do his work without having to understand it. I know now to give him permission to do what he wants, knowing for sure that whatever it is will be good and no matter what happens in the moment, whether I end up laughing or crying or not feeling anything at all, I'll be better for it after. It's important that you know that in this encounter with the Spirit, the person who was praying for me never said a word that I could hear. Of course, there are times we need to pray so those we're praying for can hear us, and be blessed by that, but equally, we don't always need to speak – we can let God do the work and the speaking. In this case, the person simply felt that God told her she needed to pray for me, inviting his presence to come and do what only he can do, so that's what she did. I was aware of her praying in tongues under her breath, but otherwise she simply laid her hand on me, blessing what God was doing. When we were finished, she just smiled at me, gave me a hug and left. As I said, this was a powerful encounter for me and after some time of the Spirit working in me, I thanked him for what he was doing (because that's polite) and asked if there was anything he wanted me to know or understand about it. I felt him say something very clearly – and I know this sounds weird – but I heard him say, "Becky, I'm sewing your arms back on."

This was the third time over about five years that I felt God showed me through a physical picture what he was doing for me spiritually. The first time was again at New Wine, maybe six years ago. After a full week of worship and being in God's presence, I heard God say to me (again I know this sounds weird and a bit like Frankenstein's monster) that over the past week he had removed the duct tape that had been holding the two halves of my brain together...

Another time, at a New Wine "Third Person" training day at St Mary's Bryanston Square, after allowing the Spirit to work on me, I felt he said that he was doing surgery on my intestine. He'd stitched up half of a long wound and he said that was enough for the time being. That bit needed to heal up and then he would carry on.

So, when God told me that he was sewing my arms back on, he went on to tell me that I had been blown apart when my sister died, like I had stepped on a landmine, but since that time, he had been putting me back together bit by bit – restoring me, as I allowed him to. For many years, I hadn't allow him to touch that part of my life as I was too frightened to face it, but once I began to open up, he started his work of restoration.

When he removed the tape that was holding the two halves of my brain together, he was reintegrating the part of me that I had detached from and denied in order to cope with what had happened. The tape represented my attempt to hold myself together, but only God could reconnect and restore the two parts of myself into one. When he did that, I was finally able to fully accept myself and believe that God wasn't mad at me. My thinking could be renewed and I could then receive his gift of hope, because once I was able to accept what had happened and see it from his perspective, which I couldn't do when I refused to acknowledge it, I could hear him speak his redemption into the situation and believe it.

When he was doing surgery on my intestines, I believe he was closing up the wound in me that meant although I knew God and was open to his Spirit, I quickly lost the effects of his filling – the spiritual nourishment he was giving me. The trauma I had experienced and then the guilt that I lived with had wounded me in a way that meant I found it hard to retain the good things – the love, the joy, the peace, that God filled me with whenever I allowed him to. By stitching up that wound, God was healing me so I wouldn't so quickly lose the effects of his good works in my life. Once he had done work on my mind, then on my innermost being, I was ready to have my arms sewn back on. He restored my thinking and he restored my spirit and then he restored my ability to give and receive from others.

God is still restoring me – I haven't heard anything about my legs yet, but then it was only recently that I "got my arms back" and I've needed time to get used to using those!

What work of restoration is the Spirit doing in you? It could be that you just need a good cleaning, like a painting that needs the accumulated dirt and grime removed so the true beauty of it can be seen. You may simply need to ask God to search your heart and see if there is any offensive way in you – turn fully to Him, ask him to purify your heart, your attitudes, tell him you're sorry where you've got it wrong, receive his forgiveness and ask for his help to do better next time. That's how we're cleansed of the dirt and grime of the world. It could be though, that there is a more serious work of restoration God is wanting to do in you. It could be that like me, you need your mind touched and renewed so God can show you things from his perspective and your thinking can be filled with his hope and life. It could be that, like me again, you need a wound from your past stitched up so that when the Spirit fills you, you can hold on to the goodness of it longer. It could be that like me, you need God to commission you for service and connection. At some point, your capacity to give and receive was damaged and you need God to come and restore that. You may even feel that, like me, you've been blown apart. There is hope. However much we feel that we have been damaged, God is able to heal us.

God longs to restore us so that we can enjoy his salvation. More than that, he longs to restore us so that we can join him in an adventure. There are works prepared for us that are beyond anything we can imagine. As we grow in security and confidence, we can step out of the boat and join him on the water.

Endnotes

1. *So Long, Insecurity: You've Been a Bad Friend to Us*, Beth Moore (Tyndale House, 2016).

2. In her book, Beth Moore has a helpful list of some of the roots of insecurity:

- *Instability in the home* (including various types of abuse, divorce, substance abuse by a parent, mental or physical illness in the home, financial instability).
- *Significant loss* (of a person, a home, a relationship).
- *Rejection* (from a parent, friend, spouse, child, boyfriend or girlfriend).
- *Dramatic change* (accident, financial crisis, even positive changes like a new baby).
- *Personal limitations* (learning disability, physical handicap, scar, acne).
- *Personal disposition and temperament* (by this she means that some people are just more sensitive and tender-hearted which makes them more vulnerable to insecurity because they take things harder and deeper to the heart than others).
- *Our culture* and the pressure it puts on all of us to be young and beautiful.
- *Pride* – she adds this because, "no outside force has the power to betray and mislead us the way our egos do. Pride talks us out of forgiving and steers us away from risking." And most importantly, "pride cheats us of intimacy, because intimacy requires transparency." If we are insecure and frightened of rejection, we will not be able to be transparent.

"Stepping Out"

What does a lifestyle of joining with Jesus on the water look like?
You're going to get wet hair...

———

Chapter 10
Life Outside the Boat

There was once a vicar's wife who lived in a remote area of the country. One day, she received a letter informing her that the Bishop would like to conduct a visit of all of the churches in that region, and asking for permission to stay with them in their vicarage for the whole week. She was horrified at the thought of hosting him for such a long time, but agreed and began making preparations.

So that her children didn't undo all of her good work, she left a note in the pantry. "This cake is for the Bishop's visit – do not eat it!" On the door of the guest bedroom she wrote, "I've cleaned this room – find somewhere else to play!" No detail escaped her notice and, finally, everything was made ready.

The week seemed to pass uneventfully and, with great relief, she waved the Bishop farewell as he left. On entering the guest bedroom to change the sheets though, the vicar's wife was surprised to see that the stack of towels she'd set out for the Bishop hadn't been touched, even though he had been with them a whole week.

As she picked up the stack of towels to put them away, a note fell out. In her own handwriting it read, "If you touch these towels, I'll break your neck..."

If you don't know someone very well, it's easy to take things the wrong way. The end of the passage that we've been considering is well-known. Peter, walking on the water, takes his eyes off of Jesus and begins to sink. He has to be rescued by the Lord, who says to him, *"You of little faith, why did you doubt?"* (Matthew 14:31). When you read that, what tone of voice do you think that Jesus used?

The answer that you instinctively give probably says a lot about the image of God that most defines your relationship with him. If you hear a rebuke in Jesus' voice, you are far less likely to take risks in the future, for fear that you would only reveal the inadequacy of your faith. I've come to believe, however, that Jesus was pleased that Peter had joined him on the water. Far from being a rebuke for the weakness of his faith, Jesus' words in verse 31 are, I think, an affectionate encouragement for Peter to have greater faith in the future.

You're going to get wet hair!

The only way to walk on water is to begin by stepping out of the boat, but don't expect it to be straightforward. Following Jesus into the impossible is something in which we have to grow. The disciples didn't get it right first time, and nor will we. Our faith in his power isn't what it should be, but it will only grow if we step out and start to trust him for things that we can't achieve in our own power.

Even seeing where he is at work so that we can join in doesn't come naturally. We have to learn how to receive, understand, test and respond to revelation. All of these things are part of the process of being taught by the Spirit and being led into a supernatural lifestyle. The way that we grow is through taking small steps and gradually increasing in faith. This is what Jesus meant when he spoke about being "faithful in the little things" in order to be entrusted with "greater things".[1]

As we go on, our progress in that adventure will depend on the extent to which we allow him to deal with the barriers of head and heart with which we struggle. Sustaining a healthy, life-long, Spirit-filled discipleship that continues to bear fruit requires us also to co-operate with the renewal of our minds and the restoration of our hearts. We can't take the outward journey of ministry and fruitfulness without the inward journey of healing and transformation.

If we're serious about following Jesus then we shouldn't settle for an impaired experience of being his disciples. He wants us all to know the joy of walking with him in things that once seemed impossible to us. This joy is so great that we must not let pride prevent us from co-operating. As Becky said in her chapters, often we will need others to hear us and help us. Our lives are sometimes shaped by painful events which are too large for the mere passage of time to "heal all things". Denying that they have affected us keeps us prisoners. For some, the negative influences that have been at work have shaped their lives over many years – we must not expect to be free from their effects overnight. There will be a process of receiving healing and learning to truly depend on God.

———

Peter sinks and has to be rescued, but we mustn't let that blind us to the truths in the verses.

Firstly, note that when Peter stepped out of the boat, he wasn't given (and didn't wait for) perfect conditions. The wind was still strong (verse 30), which meant that the waves were still crashing against them. The wind only died down when Jesus and Peter climbed back into the boat (verse 32).

Secondly, Peter actually did walk on water. If he had stepped out of the boat and immediately sank without a trace, which is what science would expect, then there would be no story here. *This incident is not recorded to tell us that walking on water is impossible.* It draws our attention to Jesus' identity, but not by saying, "Jesus can walk on water; you can't." Rather, it invites us to see Jesus as the one who can walk on water and who, if we trust him and look to him, has power to enable us to do the same! The story tells us that with him, all things are possible for us – if we keep our eyes fixed upon him. Peter's mistake was not in stepping out of the boat; it was his inability to maintain his focus on Jesus whilst he was doing something supernatural. The wind and the waves played on the doubts that surfaced from his mind and heart.

Finally, and most importantly, Jesus didn't abandon Peter. We read that Peter, *"Beginning to sink, cried out, 'Lord, save me!' Immediately Jesus reached out his hand and caught him"* (verses 30-31). There's incredible beauty in that simple word, "immediately". We see that the Lord was watching Peter all of the way, perhaps even that he was well aware that Peter's faith could falter at any time, and that he was ready to intervene when needed.

Peter's experience is full of encouragement for us. Following this incident in Matthew 14, Jesus resumes his ministry of healing (14:34-36), deliverance (14:21-28) and provision (14:29-39), together with increasing opposition (15:1-20, 16:1-12). Then he took his disciples to Caesarea Philippi, where Peter finally makes the great confession, *"You are the Christ, the Son of the living God"* (16:16).

In response, Jesus speaks about Peter's ministry: *"You are Peter, and on this rock I will build my church, and the gates of Hades will not overcome it. I will give you the keys of the kingdom of heaven; whatever you bind on earth will be bound in heaven, and whatever you loose on earth will be loosed in heaven"* (Matthew 16:18-19). Although far from the finished article at this point, as we read through the gospels and into Acts, the Lord's love and patience continue to shine through. He never gives up on Peter and this impetuous, unpredictable man becomes eventually the "Rock" that Jesus had declared him to be when he first called him (John 1:42). Peter isn't just transformed, he is given authority and a task.

Discipleship is more than being saved and healed. Yes, God wants to restore his image within us, but that includes our being able to act as his stewards on the earth. When Jesus calls us, he promises salvation and healing, but he also plans to use us to touch the lives of others. In terms of our passage in Matthew 14, life with Jesus is not merely to be experienced within the boat, but also outside it – with him on the surface of the lake. Jesus made that explicit when he first called the disciples in Mark 3:14-15, *"that they might be with him and that he might send them out to preach and to have authority to drive out demons."*

Add to that the promise of Psalm 121:8: *"The Lord will watch over your coming and going both now and evermore."* There is always a rhythm with the Lord of enjoying intimacy with him and receiving authority and commission from him. The safety of the boat is something to which we need regularly to return, but the Lord often steps away, onto the waters, and bids us follow him.

There is so much more that we can experience of him if we only choose to step out. The great English preacher, C.H. Spurgeon, once said, "Oh, brethren, be great believers!

Little faith will bring your souls to Heaven, but great faith will bring Heaven to your souls."[2]

In February 2017, over 400 whales were stranded on a New Zealand beach. It's tragic to see these magnificent creatures lying helpless and dying on the sand. Communities mobilise to try and return them to the sea before it is too late, but why do they beach in the first place? Scientists have advanced over 200 separate theories without coming to a definitive answer. Some say that underwater earthquakes damage the whales' ability to navigate, some that the whales are confused by the sonar of military submarines, others point to sunspot activity, magnetic-field activity, oil industry air guns, and so on. There is one especially simple theory though. Some suggest that the pod of whales was chasing a school of sardines, a favourite food. Naturally, the sardines can manoeuvre in shallow water, whereas the whales find themselves drawn in too close and are left at the mercy of the tide, which washes them onto the beach.[3]

It would only compound the tragedy of their deaths if it transpired that they died because they were chasing tiny fish like sardines. Like them, you and I were made for greater things. We have a dignity and place in God's purposes that is breathtaking. We are called *to reign with him in life*.[4] We are now his stewards and heirs of eternal life. And we're charged with declaring and demonstrating his kingdom to all people. Let's not waste our lives chasing after smaller things, especially when there's so much more of God that we could discover. Jesus is always going to the last, the least and the lost, and calls us to join him.

"Whoever serves me must follow me; and where I am, my servant also will be. My Father will honour the one who serves me." (John 12:26)

That is an adventure that few of us have yet to discover.

One of the most popular Christian songs of recent years is Hillsong United's "Oceans (Where Feet May Fail)".[5] The opening words, "You call me out upon the water..." place us right in Peter's situation. I believe that, in part, that song's popularity stems from capturing a deep desire within the heart of every believer for that intimacy with Jesus that is found only outside the boat.

He is calling us out upon the water. Know that he is faithful and able, and look for him to lead you. We will discover more of him outside the boat than we ever did within it.

Endnotes

1. The Parable of the Talents (Matthew 25:21) and Parable of the Ten Minas (Luke 19:17).
2. Quoted in the classic devotional, *Streams in the Desert*, L. B. Cowman (1939).
3. I first heard this illustration in a sermon given by Jacqui Kean, at that time our youth worker at All Saints' Woodford Wells.
4. Romans 5:17.
5. "Oceans (Where Feet May Fail)" by Matt Crocker, Joel Houston, Salomon Ligthelm. From the album "Zion" (Hillsong Music/Sparrow Records, 2013).

About the Authors

Paul and Becky lead All Saints' Woodford Wells in North East London, where they have been since 1995. Paul is National Leader of New Wine England, and Becky is a member of the New Wine National Leadership Team. They are both involved in leadership training for renewed churches and regularly speak at conferences in the UK and Europe.

By the same author

Jesus promised that we would grow into fullness of life by His Spirit. Like many things in life, that growth is not linear, but happens in seasons and cycles. Neither is there simple set of steps to follow guaranteeing maturity – that would be too impersonal for a God who loves relationship. Instead, spiritual growth comes from understanding some basic spiritual truths more and more profoundly. We come back to the same places again and again, each time experiencing them more deeply. This simple, but profound approach to growing in God will reinvigorate your faith and answer many questions about how to develop a vibrant spiritual life.

"Reading this book re-ignites my longing for intimacy with God and my understanding of how to keep on maturing."
JOHN COLES, Chair of Trustees, New Wine

"A must read. Paul writes from authentic and fruitful experience."
ROBBY DAWKINS, Pastor, Speaker & Bestselling Author

"A great tool for anyone wanting to go deeper in their relationship with God."
NICOLA NEAL, Founder & CEO, Revelation Life